High Meadow

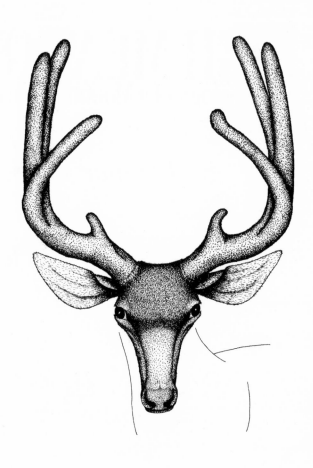

HIGH MEADOW
The Ecology of a Mountain Meadow

by *Eleanor B. Heady*

and

Harold F. Heady

A W. W. NORTON BOOK

Published by

GROSSET & DUNLAP, INC., NEW YORK

A National General Company

Books by Eleanor B. Heady

COAT OF THE EARTH

JAMBO, SUNGURA

WHEN THE STONES WERE SOFT

BRAVE JOHNNY O'HARE

TALES OF THE NIMIPOO

HIGH MEADOW (with Harold F. Heady)

Library of Congress Catalog Card No. 79–105736

ISBN: 0-448-21388-5 (Trade)
0-448-26159-6 (Library)

To the memories of our pioneer fathers
who taught us to love the world of nature.

Contents

Preface

Ecology is a word we hear on every hand. Many young readers have only vague notions of what it means.

In this brief story of one mountain meadow, we have tried to show how plants, animals, and man react upon each other and how they are affected by weather. We take our audience back into time to show the meadow forming to make its particular shape and soil..

Without the interaction of weather, water, soil, plants, animals, and man, the meadow as we know it could not live. The study of these complex organisms and forces working together as a complete whole is called *ecology*.

The future of our natural surroundings may well depend upon a knowledge of ecology and the application of that knowledge to problems of our environment.

This book represents the combined efforts of two people. Harold has a lifelong interest and profession in the natural sciences and in writing about them. Eleanor has a continuing interest in writing for young people. Harold furnished many of the ideas and much of the scientific data. He also drew the pictures and diagrams explaining scientific concepts and processes. The written words are Eleanor's.

We are greatly indebted to many friends and associates at the University of California at Berkeley for interest in, and help with, this project. We wish to give special thanks to Professors Paul J. Zinke and Marshall White of the School of Forestry and Conservation, to Professor Woodrow W. Middlekauff of the Department of Entomology, and to Mr. Brian Michael Fitzpatrick of the Sagehem Creek Experiment Station, all of whom furnished us with specialized information.

Eleanor B. Heady
Harold F. Heady

Berkeley, California
May, 1969

List of Illustrations

List of Illustrations

"Nothing exists from whose nature some effect does not follow."

Baruch Spinoza, 1632–1677

1

The Meadow Forms

Here in the mountains lies the meadow: still, snow-muffled in winter, singing with birds in springtime, ahum with bees and quivering with butterflies in summer.

Here the shy doe brings her fawn, to drink from the brook and to frolic at evening. Here the clumsy black bear digs for grubs and roots; the tiny blind mole throws up his hills and ridges on the earth.

In this favored spot the beavers build their dam.

The first flowers of spring bloom in the sun.

Later, with the coming of summer, campers pitch their tents and build their fires beside the stream. They trample the grass and break the stream banks, muddying the water.

Fishermen follow the stream, casting their lines for the rainbow and speckled trout.

In late summer and autumn, when the aspens quiver golden in the sun, hunters come to shatter the peace with booming guns.

The meadow is a place of abundant life: growing plants, animals which feed upon them and upon each other. All meadow life is attuned to the weather and the changing seasons. It is never the same from one day to the next.

The living meadow is the outgrowth of the past and all that has happened here through the ages. This is a past reckoned in millions of years by *geologists,* scientists who study the earth's surface and its changes.

Long ago, in the dim past of geologic time, the climate where our meadow lies was very cold. Snow fell and piled in drifts hundreds of feet deep. The tremendous weight of the snow packed it down into a thick layer of ice.

At the same time, ice covered much of North America. This period in geologic history is known as the Great Ice Age.

Because of their weight on the mountains, the ice layers, or *glaciers,* began to move downhill. Their descent was speeded by a slow warming of the climate, so that they melted around their lower edges and slipped downhill even faster. In warm times the ice moved fast, but the return of cold weather slowed its advance. This was not the sliding speed of an avalanche, but a very gradual movement, occurring over many hundreds of years.

As the glaciers moved, they took with them great boulders and smaller rocks that were frozen to their undersides. These stones, large and small, are known as *glacial debris*. With their stone-encrusted undersides, glaciers acted like giant sandpaper as they scoured their way downhill. These frozen giants scooped great depressions into the earth as they slid slowly down the mountains.

A glacier containing boulders and smaller particles moves more slowly than one made mostly of clean ice. Glaciers advance at varying rates. Geologists have calculated that one bit of ice, or one stone embedded in that ice, would take nearly five hundred years to travel ten miles.

This estimate is based on actual measurements of the ice movement on Switzerland's Aletsch Glacier near the summit of the Jungfrau, a high mountain in the Alps.

In Alaska many glaciers move more rapidly. On summer days when the air is warm and the sun shines twenty-four hours, the Muir Glacier often moves seven feet. During summer, Alaska's Child Glacier has been known to slide downhill thirty feet in twenty-four hours.

The great moving glacial mass dug into the sides of the mountains. Great quantities of rock were removed and transported downhill. Then, as the ice slowly melted at the forward edges, the glaciers deposited the rocks in semicircles called *glacial moraines*, often around the lower sides of bowl-like depressions. The moraines acted as dams. Sometimes the upstream walls of these bowls, or *cirques*, were high and steep, sometimes more gently sloping.

Our meadow began as a cirque scooped out by a glacier at an elevation of six thousand feet in the western United States.

As the ice continued to melt, water ran down the mountain, forming a lake behind the morainal dam at the lower edge of the cirque.

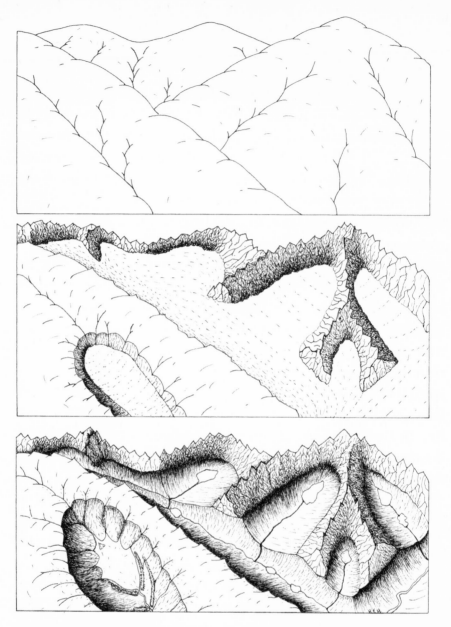

The glaciers changed the mountains. Upper diagram shows the mountains before the glaciers came. Center shows glaciers at work, ice over lower slopes with peaks above scooped into jagged outlines. In the lower diagram we see the land with the glaciers gone, leaving deep U-shaped valleys with cirques, or bowls, containing lakes. These lake basins fill in to become meadows.

Slowly, through thousands of years, the climate grew warmer. Water running down the mountain tore bits of sand from the rock surfaces and carried them into the lake. Alternating freezing and thawing cracked and crumbled the stone. Winds blew against the mountain, wearing the rock, and dislodging loose pieces.

Dust particles carried by the wind lodged against roughened rocks on the mountainsides. Then the first plants appeared, growing in tight mats with their roots clinging to the stony surfaces. These were the *crustose lichens*, crusty gray-green, gray, brown, and yellowish patches that seemed to grow as parts of the rocks themselves.

Lichens are unusual plants. When it rains they grow rapidly, absorbing water like sponges. Then during a dry spell they shrivel, until they appear to be completely dead. But with the return of water, they grow again. Lichens can live in the very cold temperatures of winter. Nor are they destroyed when the burning summer sun beats against the rocks to which they are anchored.

With the coming of the lichens, more dust caught in their rough surfaces and against the rocks where they clung. This dust brought *nitrogen* to nourish the plants. The crusty mats grew faster.

These lichens secreted, or gave off, a gas, *carbon dioxide*, which combined with water to form a weak acid. This acid ate into the rock surfaces, causing the outer layers to soften and crumble.

Lichens growing on the rocks of the mountainside helped turn the solid stone to soil, so that wind and water could carry it to the lake basin below.

All of the processes which work together to break rock into smaller and smaller particles are known as *weathering*.

Bits of sand, weathered from the surrounding rocks, were washed and blown down the mountain.

The climate warmed still more. Water flowed into the lake rapidly, filling it to overflowing. Water cascaded over the top of the dam. Then, as snow continued to melt from the mountain, the water rushed over the dam, cutting a groove, or passage, into the lowest place. Through this outlet a stream leaped down the mountainside.

Back from the shore of the lake, plants took root. Seeds brought in by birds and blown by wind settled to earth and sprouted in the rocky soil almost as soon as the ice melted.

Out in the lake, water plants began to grow. Very gradually they came, moving from warmer climates at lower elevations. Plant seeds came in the mud on the feet of animals and birds. Seeds stuck to feathers and fur.

Animals came to the lake shore. Ducks and geese settled on the water and were joined by their smaller waterfowl cousins and the shore birds.

Trout swam up the stream, leaping the rapids at the lake outlet. In the larger body of water they found a favorable home, feeding upon the insects which crawled, flew, and hopped up the mountain.

Burrowing gophers, moles, scampering mice, ground squirrels, striped chipmunks, snakes—all came to live in the fringe of plants around the lake shore.

New tracks appeared on the margins of the lake, large five-toed tracks of Stone Age men. They hunted the birds

Ducks came to the lake.

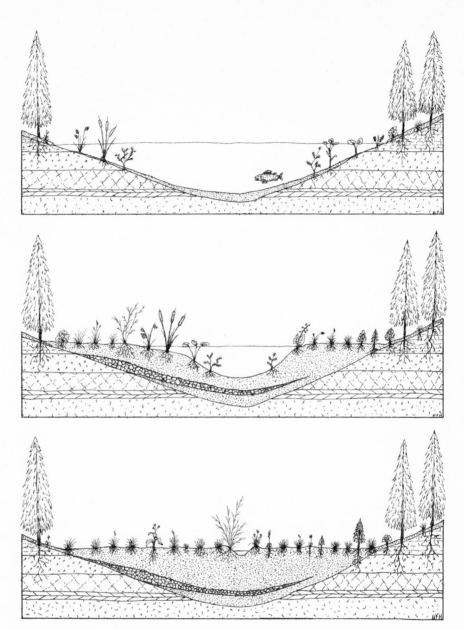

Plant succession. The upper cross-section diagram shows the partly-filled lake with water plants near shore and other plants and trees farther back. In the center diagram, we see the partly filled lake with plants growing where there was once open water. In the lower diagram the lake has disappeared, leaving a stream running across a meadow. The lake bed has filled with soil and is covered with plants.

and animals. They fished for trout at the outlet of the lake.

As the plant cover thickened, the larger animals came. Bears hunted for insects, mice, berries, and mushrooms. Deer climbed the mountain, nibbling the new shrubs as they came. Close behind them followed the *carnivores,* or meat eaters, stalking and killing the smaller animals. These included bobcats, mountain lions, and mountain coyotes.

At the same time, a slow process known as *plant succession* began changing the lake. At the very edge of the water, waves lapped the shore, washing and rolling sand and gravel down into the lake basin. This movement of the water and the lake bottom made it impossible for plants to take root near the shoreline.

A little farther out, where the water movement was more gentle, *hydrophytes,* water-loving plants, began to grow. These were submerged, or completely covered with water. Most of them had their roots anchored in the sand or mud of the lake bottom. Because these plants needed light to grow successfully, they rooted in a zone, or band, around the lake where the water was shallow enough for some light to reach them.

The circle where the submerged plants grew was a watery, tangled garden of stems, leaves, and roots. These plants varied in size, from tiny floating green specks that could be seen only with a microscope, to plants with many stems and branches that covered areas of ten or more feet. Among these plants were submerged buttercups, eelgrass with its long narrow leaves, and strange, insect-eating bladderworts.

Year after year, as the submerged plants grew, they

helped change the lake. Sand and gravel eroded, or weathered away, from the higher mountains around were washed in by streams and by rains. The tangled roots of the submerged hydrophytes caught this sand. Soil built up rapidly where these plants grew. Plants died and sank to the bottom.

Animals, insects, and fish living in the water added their dead and decaying bodies to the mass of rock and plant debris. The lake bottom built up.

Gradually, as the water became too shallow next to the shore for them to grow properly, the submerged plants moved toward the center of the lake into deeper water.

As the submerged plants moved out, others were taking their place. At first these new plants were mixed with the submerged growers, but finally took the whole zone as their own.

These were the floaters. They grew in water four to six feet deep. Firmly rooted in the mud of the lake bottom, they spread by stout *rhizomes,* underground stems which root and send up shoots at joints, or *nodes.* Unlike the submerged plants, the floaters grew with their leaves on top of the water. Water lilies spread their glossy green pads in a shining mat, perfuming the air with waxy white and yellow blossoms. Among them grew pondweeds and other floaters.

The floating plants increased and, with their leafy blanket, darkened the water below. The few remaining submerged plants, which needed light to grow, moved out into deeper water, where their cycle of growth and decay started over again.

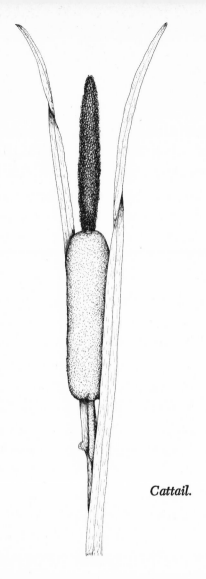

Cattail.

The floaters filled the water with a tangle of stems. They slowed the action of the waves. Soil washed in by streams, spring thaws, and rain caught among the stems. Ever so slowly, this soil settled to the bottom. Helping to fill the lake still more were dead parts of these bulky plants, along with the dead bodies of insects, fish, and animals which lived and died in and around the lake. These plant and animal remains were partly decayed, or decomposed, by minute *bacteria* living in the water. Plants, animals, weathering—all worked together to build up the bottom of the lake.

Now the floaters found the water too shallow. They moved gradually out toward the lake center, invading the zone of submerged plants. The submerged plants moved again into deeper water.

As the lake margins became shallower, a new group crowded in among the floaters. Finally, tall swamp plants covered the area completely. These were bulrushes, cattails, and reeds, tough-leaved and growing six or more feet tall. A tangled mass of leathery thick roots, rhizomes, covered the mud with a knotty carpet and shaded the shallow water. The zone nearest the lake shore became a swamp.

The thick growth of swamp plants caught and held the rock debris washed into the lake. Dying leaves and stems from the giant reeds and cattails fell into the water. The lake bottom built up rapidly, making the water still shallower. It became an unfriendly *habitat*, or home, for the swamp plants.

As the water level lowered, the reeds, bulrushes, and cattails moved out into deeper water. Into their former territory came new plants. These were the sedges and small rushes. Sedges are tough, with leaves and stems that look like grass. The rushes, too, resemble coarse grasses. A mass of slender roots and rhizomes crowded the soil.

Where open water once lapped the sandy lake shore there was dry land. Spring flooding made the soil very wet. Other plants joined the sedges and rushes. Blue flag, or wild

Wire grass, a small rush growing in wet soil.

Blue flag or wild iris.

iris, dotted the green with pale blue flowers. Marsh marigold glowed yellow amid the tangle of leaves. Mints, bluebells, or campanulas, and violets all added color to the green lake margins.

Very gradually these plant groups, or communities, grew, each pushing the one ahead of it farther toward the center of the lake. At the same time, communities following one another changed the habitat, or place where they grew. This habitat change made ideal conditions for the next group of plants to take over. This changing of plant communities, one following another, is called *plant succession*.

While a succession of plant communities helped fill the lake, the stream continued to flow down the mountain. It brought sand weathered from the rocks above. This sand washed into the lake and spread out in a fanlike delta. Where the current rushed in, with its load of sand, plants could not root. An uneven area of sandy soil built up.

From the valleys below came the winds, blowing from west to east across the lake. Where the waves washed against the eastern shore, few plants took root. The wave action rolled sand into the lake, cutting a pocket back into the shore. The action of wind and water caused the lake to become an uneven basin.

Finally, after hundreds, or even thousands, of years, the lake disappeared, filled completely with sand washed from the surrounding mountains and with the remains of the plants and animals which lived in and upon it. The stream rushing down the mountain flowed as a meandering creek across a meadow.

Spring rains rushed down the stream, cutting the channel deeper. The water level, or table, within the meadow soil dropped still lower. The soil became drier. Into the habitat of the sedges and rushes moved grasses and other small plants, leaving a few of the former community in wet places near the creek.

On higher ground above the original lake shore grew a circle of shrubs. Behind these, with their roots in drier soil, the dark pines and firs soared skyward.

Birds nested in the trees. The "whee-whee-kyuck" of the giant pileated woodpecker rang across the land. Jays filled the air with squawks, quarreling with the red squirrels, scolding anyone who could hear.

Deer crossed the open space. Coyotes hunted. Bears fished in the stream.

Sometimes, in early morning or when night darkened the space between the trees, a mountain lion padded softly from the sheltering forest.

Here Indians camped. They fished in the stream, hunted the game and set fire to the grass. The Indians helped change the meadow by trampling the soil. Their fires burned new trees and brush that crowded the borders, helping to keep the center space open.

Here, ages in the making, was the mountain meadow.

Here, today, live many animals and plants in one community. People come now as earlier people came before, hunting, fishing, seeking rest and refreshment, or perhaps only a bit of solitude.

In spring, summer, autumn, and winter, the meadow is living, growing, changing: a place of wonder.

2

The Meadow Sleeps

Winter holds the meadow in its snow-locked grip. For three months and more, storms have lashed these mountains, piling the snowdrifts thirty feet deep. At the edge of the meadow away from the sweep of the westerly winds, drifts gleam white against the dark green of firs and pines. The snow has a glazed frozen crust. Winter is old, almost at an end.

Mark Stevens, the forest ranger, comes up the stream, walking slowly on snowshoes. He skirts the edges of the frozen beaver pond, stops to watch the still expanse of white.

The tap-tap-tap of a woodpecker echoes wildly through the silence. Even in the coldest winter, these hardy birds chop into trees with their sharp beaks and send their barbed, probing tongues deep into the wood to spear grubs.

Mark chuckles to himself. "Guess he's going to make it again."

On around the frozen pond goes the ranger, moving

quietly so he won't disturb the animals and birds who have chosen this place for their winter home.

As Mark Stevens crosses the meadow between orange-yellow signs lettered *Snow Survey,* he stops every hundred feet to measure the snowfall. He pushes a long aluminum tube with a jagged cutting edge into the snow. When the tube reaches the earth below, Mark pulls it out. With hand scales he weighs the tube and the snow core it contains. He records the weight in a notebook. Then the ranger taps out the snow and proceeds on, to sample in another place.

The ranger sends his snow weights to *hydrologists,* scientists who study the water cycle. By keeping careful accounts of snow-water amounts in the mountains, these hydrologists are able to determine how much spring flooding to expect in the valleys below.

Water from snow and rain moves into and out of the meadow—and over all the earth—in a continuous cycle. Water evaporates, or rises from the surfaces of streams and lakes, from the ocean, too. Water is transpired, or given off, by growing plants whose roots have taken it from the soil. This water gathers in clouds from which it falls to the earth's surface as rain and snow.

Snow melts and with the rain, runs into streams, lakes, and finally to the ocean. Some of the water from rain and snow seeps into the soil and becomes ground water. This water is absorbed by the roots of plants or else erupts as springs at lower elevations.

Then the cycle begins again: transpiration, evaporation—together called *evapotranspiration*—sending water into the air. So the water continues to move, rising, forming

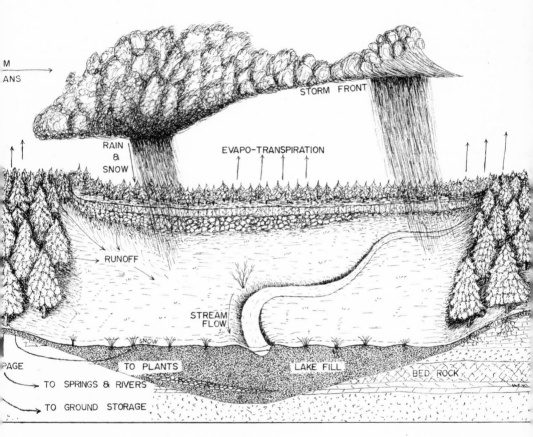

The hydrologic cycle. Water evaporates from streams, oceans, lakes, and soil, and transpires from plants. This moisture collects in clouds and falls to earth as rain and snow to flow into streams and oceans, fill lakes, and run back into the soil, shown in cross-section, beginning the cycle again.

The snowshoe hares blend their white winter coats with the landscape. Their big feet enable them to walk over the snow.

clouds and falling back to earth in a *hydrologic cycle.*

Mark Stevens studies the ground as he walks. Winter tracks of animals make a network on the old snow. He sees the three-toed track of a grouse, the round track of a bobcat, the long tracks of a snowshoe hare. Across the snowy meadow meanders the zigzag hunting trail of a fox.

The ranger bends to examine tiny tracks, the myriad crisscross trails of white-footed mice. He records what he sees in his notebook, then moves on and out through the trees at the upper end of the meadow.

After the swish-swish of Mark Stevens' snowshoes retreats into the forest, a shadow moves in the willow thicket at the upper side of the beaver pond. A snowshoe hare hops out, looking timidly in all directions.

No enemies are in sight, no coyote, bobcat, or fox. No shadow of owl or hawk darkens the snow. Two more stealthy hops and the hare stops beside a shrub which pokes its spindly top through the crusted snow. He nibbles at the branch tips.

The snowshoe hare of our western mountains is sometimes called a rabbit. Hares look much like rabbits, but they differ in some very definite ways. Hares do not build nests. They live in hollowed places, or hides, in thickets of brush. Rabbits make nests.

Young hares are born fully furred. They can hop around and find food—forage—for themselves when they are barely two weeks old. Baby rabbits are naked, blind, and helpless. Hares leap, while rabbits dart and hop.

The easiest way to tell a hare from a rabbit it by its tail. Rabbits have round fluffy tails, while those of the hares are more slender and two to three inches long.

Our snowshoe hare is also called the varying hare because his color changes with the seasons. Now, in winter,
he is white except for dark eartips. Such coloring blends
with the snow around him so that the *predators*, animals
who might catch him for food, have trouble seeing him.

When an animal's color blends with his surroundings
he is said to have *protective coloring*, color which protects
him from his enemies. Many animals have such coloring.
That of the snowshoe hare is among the best.

The snowshoe hare gets his name from his snowshoe
feet. In winter he grows stiff, inch-long hairs which extend
around his feet like snowshoes. With these he can walk on
top of the snow. He is ideally adapted for winter living,
with color that hides him from his enemies and snowshoes
that take him easily over the surfaces of the deepest drifts.
The hare's food of twigs and buds is seldom covered by
winter's snow. Only an ice storm which glazes all the plants
keeps him from getting his meals.

The sun beats against the trees along the north side
of the meadow. With a "plop," a blob of half-melted snow
falls from a fir branch into the drift below. Before the
echoes have died away, the snowshoe hare darts back into
his hide beneath the willows. Caution, along with color,
helps him to survive among many enemies.

Around the fringes of the pond, bark-stripped willow
branches rise above the snow. The buds are gone, eaten
entirely by the snowshoe and his kin. The bark is chewed
almost down to the snow line. Even the tips of small
branches are missing.

Willows are tough strong-growing shrubs, or small trees. If it were not for the constant winter pruning of bark-eating hares and their cousins the cottontail rabbits, willows would grow over more of the meadow. Because the animals are there to keep the willows trimmed they do not spread throughout the damp places so as to change the meadow completely. The hares and rabbits help keep the meadow an open sunny spot.

Near the upper end of the meadow, a dark shape moves over the snow. Out into the sunlight, glowing orange-red against the drifts, comes a fox. Winter is hard for him, so he hunts many hours each day. He stays awake all night to stalk his prey.

The fox sniffs the snow. Something was there. He trots downstream in a zigzag course, stopping to smell where other creatures have passed. Then, ahead of him on the snow, a shadowy shape darts toward the trees. One graceful bounding leap brings the hunter even with the fleeing animal. He pounces and a squirrel lies dead and bleeding on the snow.

From the trees a screech startles the quiet suddenness of the squirrel's death.

The fox ducks as a shining blue and black jay swoops toward him. The bird settles on the snow and pecks at the drops of blood.

Carefully, almost daintily, the killer picks up his prey. Carrying the dead squirrel in his mouth, he trots to a drift near the trees. There he drops his burden. Both front feet spraying snow, the fox digs a hole and places the dead squirrel in it. Then he rakes the snow over it and trots away.

Back to his zigzag course down the meadow goes the fox, sniffing the wind. His dark ears stand stiff and alert to hear the softest sound. He is a picture of vigilance, aglow against the snow.

Higher in the sky rises the sun, warming the snow so that it melts on top. The fox breaks through the crust, which slows his progress toward the beaver dam. Out onto the pond ice he trots, to the snow-covered mound of the beaver lodge. He sniffs all around it, walks over the top. No use. The beavers are safe and snug in their frozen palace of mud. The clever fox cannot dig through the pond ice to the open waters where the beavers swim.

At a sunny spot on a rise near the stream, the fox curls up in the snow to rest. His fluffy tail wraps around like a muffler, covering his feet and his nose. He dozes, warm in his winter finery, on his bed of snow.

Foxes, like snowshoe hares, are ideally adapted to living in cold weather. Each autumn they grow thick fine coats of fluffy underfur. Over this coat, with the stiff hairs growing through it, is the outer coat of longer hairs. It is in autumn that the beautiful tail of the fox reaches its finest. This tail grows as long as the animal's body and almost as thick. It is reddish brown with a white tip. The fox's body is heavily furred—red-brown on the back, shading to white underneath. His legs and paws blend from dark brown into black boots of stiff thick hair.

The sleeping fox stirs, uncurls his tail, sniffs his pointed nose into the wind, then leaps up and runs a crooked course across the meadow.

He stops suddenly, nose up, testing the air. One foot

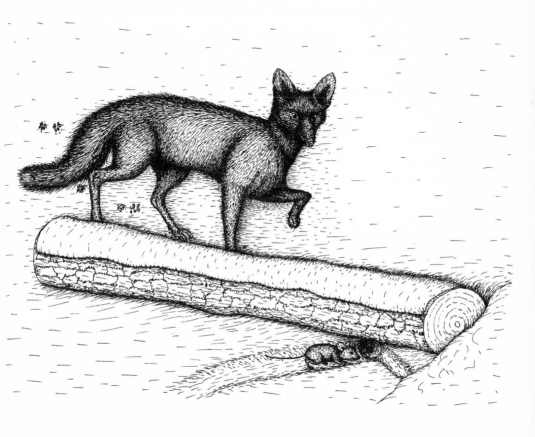

The fox stops, alert, testing the cold winter air.

lifts. Not a hair of his tawny coat moves. He springs. A terrified screech, a tussle, disturb the snow beside the willow thicket. The fox lifts the limp body of a snowshoe hare and carries it across the drifts, leaving a trail of crimson bloodstains.

Back to his cache goes the fox. He digs into the snow and brings up the buried squirrel. A soft, short bark brings another fox trotting from the shadows.

The hunter pushes the hare toward his mate. They gulp the meat, then, side by side, disappear into the brush.

So the cycle continues: hares eat willows so they are kept in balance with the rest of the meadow; foxes eat hares so there are not enough of them to destroy all the willows.

If some squirrels do not fall prey to foxes and other predators, there is danger that their hidden winter supplies of nuts and seeds may not be sufficient to keep them through the cold winter months. If there is not enough food, the squirrels may die of starvation.

The red squirrels, or chickarees, live in a nest under the roots of a tall fir tree. Here, and in other places in the meadow, they store their winter hoards of pine nuts. High in their home fir tree, wedged securely in crotches where branches grow from the tree trunk, is a supply of dried mushrooms. The squirrels prepare well for the lean season. They eat what has been saved and wait for the time when fruit, nuts, and young birds will come again to the meadow.

Under a big snowbank next to the home tree is a cache of pine nuts. The squirrels undermined this drift with a network of twisting snow tunnels. Some of the tunnels lead to their feasting places. Others simply wind around, under and through the snow. On stormy days the squirrels play hide-and-seek in their snow castle, chasing each other through its twisting passageways.

Sunny days bring the chickarees out into the treetops, where they run, leap, and chatter much as they do in summer.

A young red squirrel leaves his nest under the fir roots and dashes across the snow to one of the tunnel entrances leading down into a drift. A shadow falls upon him as the jay screeches overhead. With the jay's warning, the squirrel ducks into his burrow. The hunting fox trots on to find easier prey.

This meadow is the kingdom of the Steller's jay. He keeps order with scolding, warns of danger by squawking excitedly. Other animals hide when they hear his voice, for they know that something is coming that will upset the routine of their lives.

The jay lives in his snowy kingdom throughout the winter. He eats buds and the few insects he can find. Sometimes he discovers the winter store of a squirrel and feasts on nuts. A robber among birds, the jay eats anything he finds. Few occupants of the forest or meadow will dispute the claims of this noisy, quarrelsome, demanding bird. He attacks other birds and animals with his sharp beak. Even large creatures fear its sting.

The Steller's jay is clown of the winter. His bright blue, gray, and black feathers glisten against the snow. His black-crested head bobs up and down as he watches, shrieks, and scolds.

With a sudden whirr, a dark form bursts from the shelter of the firs and soars straight as an arrow across the meadow to the edge of the frozen beaver pond. A grouse settles beside the drooping, snow-entangled willows. Wide horny winter feet keep him from breaking through the crust. The fat brown bird pecks at willow buds, eating steadily. Then, with a roar of wings, he returns to hide in the snow beneath the trees.

The midday sun soars overhead. With a sudden plop, snow drops from a tree. Most of the animals and birds hide during bright daylight hours because they are afraid of the winter-hungry carnivores.

Shadows lengthen. At the west side of the meadow the clean white aspens shine like marble columns in the slanting rays of the sun. One dead brown leaf flutters on a high branch.

But look, something is different there. Where yesterday the branches were thin and bare, today there glisten thickened dark lumps. Buds are swelling, promise that winter will soon be over.

A dark shadow sails across the meadow. Soaring in a wide circle, on silent, soft-feathered wings, the great horned owl is hunting, his powerful talons spread ready to grab any scuttering mouse or squirrel.

Cottontail rabbits and snowshoe hares hide in the willow thicket, trembling as the sinister shadow glides above them.

This largest of all the owls hunts while his mate takes her turn on the nest. For these are winter-nesting birds. Too lazy to build for themselves, the horned owls took an

The great horned owl takes his turn sitting on the eggs.

abandoned hawk's nest. The untidy bowl of sticks lodged in a tall, dead pine was enlarged and remodeled to suit the new owners.

Because their eggs are laid in winter and the young hatch while snow is still on the ground, the nest must be very warm. The parent birds line the nest with feathers which they pull from their own breasts, enough to make a warm covering over the eggs. Then, as another precaution against chilling, the owls take turns sitting on the nest. Because they pluck so many of their own feathers, the parent owls have almost bare spots, like inverted saucers, on their own breasts. This "nesting patch" fits snugly down over the eggs, keeping them very warm. The nearly round, cream-colored eggs, and the young birds which hatch from them, are never left alone.

The great bird sails down, talons extended. With a faint, dying squeak an unlucky meadow mouse makes a meal for the great owl with the ears, or horns, on his head. He flies up into the tree to change places with his mate.

Dusk softens the meadow with long shadows. In the distance sounds a wailing, yipping call: sad, eerie, longing. The mountain coyote sings a twilight song, his greeting to the night. With darkness, the coyote and the great owl will be kings in this place, sharing the game with bobcats and perhaps a mountain lion.

Late winter is a lean season for the creatures of the meadow, but better times are coming. If they can survive the cold and starving months, their mountain home will be transformed into a paradise of growing things.

3

The Meadow Stirs

The wind blows softly from the southwest, melting the snow surface to a glassy glitter.

Beside the creek, slender willow stems turn pale yellow. Brown buds swell. Here and there one breaks through its brown cage to show the shining gray velvet of a pussy willow catkin.

As the days grow warmer, bare spots of wet brown earth appear near the rushing creek. Dry grass stubble, cut off by mice, sticks up like bristles. At the watery edges of melting snowbanks, fine green shoots sprout like emerald fringes.

Near the meadow border where a drift nestles in the shadow of a tall pine, the first flowers bloom. These snow plants, or coral roots, come at the edges of melting drifts. Up through cold, wet, decaying wood they push thick red stems. Bell-shaped red flowers open as if by magic.

Another snow-loving plant, called pinedrops, springs up nearby. It stands close to the trees, two feet tall, bearing greenish-white, drooping flowers.

These first flowers of spring are *saprophytes*, plants

Pussy willow catkins.

which grow only on decayed wood or plant material. They flower briefly, then disappear almost as quickly as they come. Out in the meadow, away from the forest edges, there are no plants of this kind. They can live only in close association with trees.

Along with the saprophytes come the mushrooms and puffballs. These are *fungi,* plants which have no green leaves. Fungi usually grow on dead or decaying plant material. Some special kinds grow on living trees. White, cream, orange, yellow, and even red or speckled, these strange plants spring up overnight or in a very few hours. They dot the margins of snowbanks. Shiny mushroom buttons decorate logs and cluster at the bases of trees.

Mushrooms, toadstools, puffballs—the large and varied group of fungi—provide favorite delicacies for many forest and meadow animals.

From the shelter of the woods glides a big black bear. Close behind her waddle two furry cubs.

The tiny cubs, one black and the other brown, were born during the winter. Secure in her hidden den, the female bear *hibernated,* or slept. There she bore her young and nursed them until they were about two months old. Then mother bear knew that the weather had warmed and it was time to leave the security of her hiding place. The cubs' eyes were open. They became restless in the crowded confines of their den. The old bear grew uneasy too, for she was hungry. So she broke through the covering of leaves and brush that she had pulled so carefully over the opening last autumn, and led her children proudly into the wide world.

When the bears reach the open meadow, the big bear stands up on her hind legs and looks around. She sniffs the air, first in one direction, then another. Her keen nose smells for enemies or food. Perhaps she smells those delicious mushrooms.

Mother bear growls softly. The cubs follow her toward the creek, out where the snow has melted. The old bear begins to eat new grass. First the brown cub, then the black, nibble uncertainly at these strange green shoots.

The old bear waddles, flat-footed and wary, toward a decaying log at the forest's edge. The cubs follow, wandering from the straight path to investigate a fluttering moth and a fresh earth mound thrown up by a pocket gopher. A low "whuff" from mother brings the two youngsters at a wobbly gallop.

There, close to the log, the old bear digs at a circle of white-capped mushrooms. She eats eagerly, then pushes some toward the cubs. They crowd each other to taste this new pungent food. Now they will know how to look for mushrooms, too. Thus the mother bear shows her children where to find what is good to eat.

Bears will eat almost anything. We call such animals *omnivorous*. When the bears first awake from their winter sleep, or hibernation, they often eat the flesh of large animals, such as deer, which have died of starvation during the winter. They also catch and eat mice, turn stones to get insects hiding beneath them, and eat all kinds of fruit and berries, as well as the bulbs of certain plants.

Suddenly, the bears stop digging. Mother growls softly. The black cub, then his smaller brown sister, dash

The frightened cub watches from the safety of the tree.

to a dead pine and climb swiftly. At the foot of the tree, the old bear stands guard.

From behind the rock pile below the beaver dam slinks a long golden animal. He is the cougar, or mountain lion.

The female bear knows he will catch and kill her cubs if he can. She growls, warning the big cat. He advances stealthily, listening between steps, yellow-green eyes aglitter. Winter has been hard for the big cat. Hunger gnaws his stomach.

The bear moves toward the killer cat. The cougar hesitates, then swerves to the left, never taking his eyes from the furry hulk of the angry bear. Neck hair bristling, the bear charges.

But the agile cat is gone. The forest closes around him. He will wait until darkness, then try again.

Perched in the tree the cubs watch, round-eyed, waiting for their mother's soft, grunting "all clear."

First the brown cub, then the black one, back down the tree trunk. Out into the sunny center of the meadow they scamper. The old bear shuffles after them.

Again the big bear calls. She digs with strong front claws, throwing the dirt to one side, tearing at roots. Up comes a white bulb, a sweet dogtooth violet. The mother bear gives it to the smallest cub, then digs furiously for another for the black cub. They chew the crunchy morsels, another good new food.

The mother bear ambles down toward the beaver dam. A fallen log lies across her path. With a low, bear-talk growl, she calls the lagging cubs. They trot eagerly to her side, then scramble to the top of the log. Standing on their hind legs, the young bears push each other back and forth like two small boys.

The female bear is still very hungry. With her strong-clawed front feet she tears at a decaying stump.

The cubs roll down to watch.

Bits of wood fly, then the old bear puts her head next to the wood. Her long red tongue flicks out to lick up grubs hiding in the rotting wood. The eager youngsters rush to share the feast, their little tongues imitating that of their mother.

The female bear tears the wood to bits, scattering it

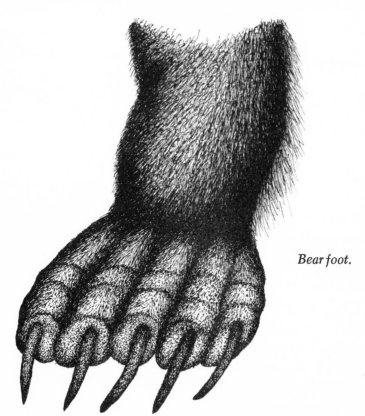

Bear foot.

over the ground. The decayed wood will become part of the meadow soil, returning organic food to nourish the plants which grow there.

Decaying of wood and plant material is caused by *bacteria,* tiny microscopic organisms which live in the soil and feed upon plant and animal materials. Thus the bacteria help turn dead material back into soil to nourish new plants.

As the days grow warmer, green plants of many kinds carpet the meadow floor. The sun, which shines for longer hours in spring, is the source of this growing. Indeed, the energy which supports all living plants and animals comes from the sun.

By a process called *photosynthesis,* plants make sugar compounds. Green *chlorophyll* in leaf cells captures the energy of the sun. This energy, combined with *carbon dioxide* from the air, and water and minerals from the soil, is changed into *carbon compounds,* or sugars. Plants use these carbon, or organic, compounds for growth and store the excess. Some carbon compounds are used by plants to make more complicated materials, such as wood fiber which strengthens stems.

When an animal eats plants, the stored organic food material digests and releases *calories,* or energy, which the animal uses.

Early warm spring days awake the chipmunks from winter hibernation. First to emerge from his burrow is a large male. He pokes his nose from a pile of brush near the willows. Under this brush hides the entrance to his underground home.

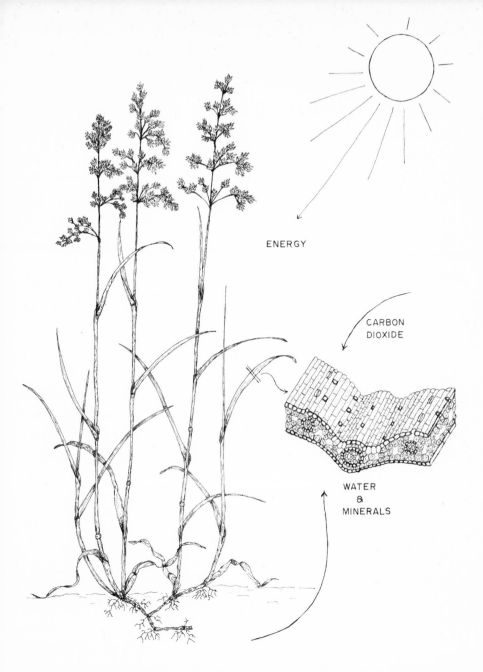

ENERGY

CARBON
DIOXIDE

WATER
&
MINERALS

Photosynthesis. Energy from the sun is captured by green chlorophyll cells in the grass leaves shown in the enlarged cross-section at right. This sun energy combines wth carbon dioxide from the air, and water and minerals from the soil, to make carbon compounds, or sugars. These sugars are used by the plant for growth. The excess, or unused carbon compounds, are stored in plant tissues.

Spring is a happy time for the chipmunks.

The chipmunk flicks his bushy tail, sits up and rubs the last bit of sleepiness from his eyes with handlike front feet. Then he scampers toward the fallen log, sniffs where the bears tore the stump, and leaps to the top.

The chipmunk looks around, flirts his tail, shakes his fur, then begins to sing. "Chuck-chuck, chuck-chuck, chuck-chuck," he trills. All the joy of life rediscovered is in his singing.

At the first joyous notes from the big chipmunk, a dozen others appear, popping up all around the meadow. They scurry to perches on logs, rocks, and stumps and join the chorus. The meadow echoes with song.

Chipmunks are perhaps the happiest of the meadow dwellers. Spring is a time for frolic and gay abandon. When they awake from winter hibernation, full granaries provide enough food. The chipmunks filled these underground storage rooms in autumn when nuts and seeds were abundant.

In spring the chipmunks seek mates, living a life of music, feasting, and lovemaking. They chase each other in playful games or sing cheerful, chuckling songs while other less provident animals search for food.

During this chipmunk spring, many of them fall prey to carnivores, hungry after the long cold winter. Perhaps chipmunks are careless during their happy time. Perhaps the hunters are fiercer.

The big chipmunk scratches his furry side with a hind foot. Then he turns around, dark stripes flashing in the sun. His dark-banded, white-fringed tail flicks happily as he trills again, "chuck-chuck-chuck," very rapidly.

The famous naturalist, Ernest Thompson Seton, listened each spring to the chipmunk chorus around his Connecticut home. Many times, he counted the trills in a chipmunk's song, and found that one little performer sang one hundred and fifty or more chirps per minute.

As the days warm, plants and trees in and around the meadow change rapidly. The willows along the stream and by the beaver pond turn slowly from dull brown to yellow-green. Buds on their stems swell, then burst brown sheaths, and the *catkins*, or blossoms, shine in the sun. These are of many kinds. Some catkins are pale greenish yellow, but scattered among them are the pussy willows, whose blossoms nestle like furry gray kittens along the branches. There are pussy willows with big catkins and others with tiny shiny flowers. The gray blossoms bloom still more to become fuzzy yellow, as the pollen-bearing *stamens* burst through the gray fur. Then the catkins turn dull brown and fall to the ground. Close behind come the first tiny pale green leaves.

The aspens beside the beaver dam grow catkins, too. These are greenish yellow and resemble little fat worms. They dangle from the trees, filling the air with the pungent odor of pollen. These blossoms are sometimes called "wigglers" because they sway and dance in the breeze. As the days warm, the catkins turn from yellow-green to brown, and they, too, fall to the ground to be followed by shimmering pale green leaves.

Spring touches the firs and pines surrounding our meadow. Firs and pines, called *conifers*, trees which do not shed their leaves, show no burst of flowers or catkins. Pale green new growth tips every branch, and tiny cones grow.

Willow catkins.

The red-brown twigs of the streamside chokecherry bushes burst into snowy blossom.

Nearer the trees, the fluffy white blooms of deer brush spread over low bushtops. Their fragrance perfumes the air.

Pale lavender violets nestle in the grass. Here and there, in damp places, the spiky leaves and graceful blue blossoms of wild iris, or flag, open to the sun. A blaze of purple-red shooting stars and the golden-yellow of dog-tooth violets dot the green with glowing color.

In every open spot of ground, grass springs up. The young shoots are tiny, almost hairlike, but with warm spring days they grow rapidly, until the whole meadow wears a green carpet. This new grass provides a feast for many of the animals. It is food for rabbits, hares, bears, deer, and countless other inhabitants of the woods and meadow. These animals, which eat grass and leaves, are called *herbivores.*

Spring in the meadow brings the birds in great flocks. Here in these mountains they build their nests and raise their broods of young.

The great pileated woodpecker, who lives here all through the winter, repairs his tree hole to make a nest. His drumming thunders through the woods. As he flies back and forth with his mate, their black pointed crests and red heads flash in the sunlight. They fly to the rotten stump where the bear feasted, peck holes in the wood, then use their long barbed tongues to spear hidden insects. Woodpeckers' tongues are ideal for this purpose, for they can be

The pileated woodpecker lives all year long in the woods by the meadow.

extended four or five inches beyond their bills to fish grubs from the deepest wood crevices.

With a rush of wings, the woodpeckers fly into the tall nesting tree. Fifty feet up, they have chiseled a hole deep into the wood. It is six to eight inches across and is carefully lined with fir bark. In this nest the female woodpecker will lay three to six white eggs.

Other birds come to the meadow. The jays build, scolding and swooping. The shy chickadees bob in and out among the pine needles or perch in the willow thicket. They are building, too, lining an abandoned woodpecker hole with bits of grass to make a soft bed for the tiny, reddish-brown, speckled eggs that will soon nestle there. The chickadees hop about, hunting insects and insect eggs.

Chickadees have large round heads, white with black caps striped with white. Their bodies are short and ball-shaped. The cheerful birds chatter and chirp as they work. But now it is spring, and sometimes there comes a pause in the usual twitter. The male chickadee sits very still and sings a sweet-sad, high-pitched love song to his mate.

The clear toy-trumpet call of the red-breasted nuthatch blends with other birdsongs. High in the trees by the meadow, a pair of these short-tailed, topsy-turvy birds hunt, either end up. Their sharp black bills peck in steady rhythm as they creep along the tree trunks.

Red-brown male juncos with black-hooded heads sing sharp, quavering songs as they hop over the ground searching for seeds left from the previous autumn. Their gray-capped mates chirp and hunt with them.

Juncos nest in holes in the earth. Thick walls of plant

stems are packed together with dried grass and moss. The birds line the nest with very fine moss to make a soft bed for their gray and brown speckled eggs, and for the naked young birds which hatch from them.

Suddenly, the chattering juncos grow silent. Overhead glides a sinister shadow, a sharp-shinned hawk hunting for his dinner. His beady eyes rake the earth as he soars on silent wings over the beaver pond and close above the willow thicket. The juncos among the willows freeze. Not a feather moves. The hawk may not see them if they are quiet.

But the hawk's eyes are keen and he is hungry. With a sudden dive he hits a crouching female junco and soars into the sky with the struggling bird clutched in his hooked talons.

On the surface of the beaver pond, a brown nose and head ripple the water as a beaver glides across, trailing a v-shaped wake. He dives suddenly, his flat tail slapping the surface of the water. The loud plop echoes from the trees. But the beaver who made the noise has ducked through the underwater entrance into his lodge.

In a few days the beaver family will leave the meadow and travel downstream to spend the summer visiting colonies of their kinfolk.

Over the snow-capped mountain, up where the meadow creek has its beginnings in melting snow, a cloud gathers. Blacker and blacker it becomes, until its shadow covers all the open space between the trees. Birdsongs cease. Chipmunks seek their burrows. Squirrels scurry to shelter in the trees.

A cool breeze sighs through the evergreens. Lightning strikes from the rocks of the mountain, blazing the meadow with a flash brighter than the sun. Crashing thunder echoes against the rocks and rolls across the land. A fierce wind blows cold down the mountain, bringing with it huge drops of rain. The rain falls faster. The air grows chill and the drops turn to slushy snow. It coats trees and shrubs. A cold dripping blanket mashes the grass and flowers.

But such a late-spring storm cannot last. The cloud passes. The sun comes from hiding and melts the snow. Meadow grasses sparkle with diamond drops of water as the sun sends its last slanting salute to the day.

A squirrel chatters and the gay male chipmunk climbs back upon his log and begins to sing. From the dead pine at the side of the meadow, the great horned owl welcomes the night, "Who-whoo, whooo-whooo, whoooooo!"

4

The Meadow Rushes

Late-spring sunshine floods the meadow with clear morning light. Chickadees sing from the treetops. Jays scold, grouse cluck. Juncos chirp and twitter.

Beside the creek a doe puts her head to the water and drinks. She raises her eyes, trembles, then, ears forward, she listens. Something is coming. Away bounds the doe to the brushpile where her hidden fawns blend their spots with the sunlight filtered through leaves and branches.

Noise of a laboring motor invades the morning. Into the clearing chugs a jeep truck, bumping over the frost-roughened track that leads up from the valley. In the back of the jeep perches a picnic table with benches attached, the kind that is common in our national forests.

Mark Stevens, the ranger, is at the wheel. Beside him sits his assistant, Jim Marshall. Mark brings the car to a sputtering halt on the smooth grassy creekside above the beaver pond. There, a stone fireplace stands as it was left by last year's campers. The two men climb from the truck and lift the table to the ground.

"Tips a little, Jim," says the ranger. "Let's boost this lower side with some flat stones."

"That should do it." Jim starts toward the rock pile beside the beaver pond.

Together the two men secure the table. Then they clean and repair the fireplace.

Mark grins. "Let's take a look around, Jim."

"Good. Wonder how all our friends made it through the winter."

"Might even find a fawn or two. Bet anything that doe we scared has young somewhere in the brush."

The ranger and his assistant walk slowly around the meadow, checking tracks, the condition of the beaver dam, earth mounds thrown up by pocket gophers and moles, the rotten log with its bear marks.

"Guess all the animals are back, Mark. See these bear tracks here in this soft dirt?"

A jay scolds from the low branch of a chaparral bush.

"That fellow wants us to leave," laughs Mark. "Come on. Let's get over the hill."

The two men climb into the jeep and clatter down the track.

The doe listens. From her hiding place in a thicket of fir trees and low snowbrush, she watches the men as they circle the meadow. She makes no movement or sound, for that could betray her hiding place and that of the fawns at her feet. They lie quietly in a mixture of sun and shadow, almost invisible, their spotted coats blending with the dappled sunshine beneath the bushes.

When the last motor sounds die away, the doe moves

cautiously toward the open space of the meadow. Her long ears point forward, alert for the slightest sound. Big dark eyes watch for movements that might betray an enemy. Then she turns her head ever so slightly toward the thicket where her fawns hide. She murmurs softly to call them.

Graceful, golden with white spots, the two youngsters trot from hiding. One of them takes a sudden turn and gallops off to be joined in an instant by the doe who herds him back with a nudge of her chin.

The fawns follow their mother to the creek's edge where she crops tender alder shoots. The doe eats a few bites of grass, then leads the fawns once again into the thicket.

From the upper end of the meadow comes a huge blacktail buck. He stands silhouetted against the dark trees, alert, watching. Above his head soar velvety summer antlers.

Deer usually hide during the warm part of the day, eating mostly in the morning and again at dusk. They drink from the creek near daybreak and at sundown. Perhaps deer know that predators are less likely to see them during these early and late hours. Or maybe they prefer to be abroad when the air is cool.

The deer of our meadow are the blacktail, or mule deer. The name comes from black tails set against white rump patches, or from their long ears, resembling mule ears. Another, and perhaps better, name for these deer is bounding blacktail, from their habit of bounding or leaping when pursued.

Ernest Thompson Seton tells of seeing a herd of black-

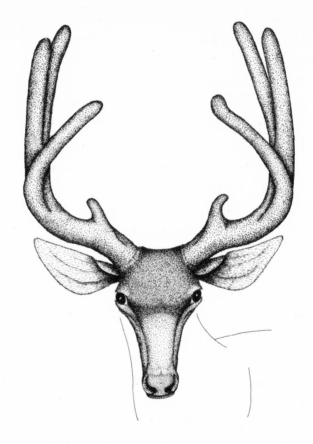

The wide-antlered buck with horns in summer velvet.

tails completely elude a pursuing pack of hounds by bound-ing from one rise to the next. Hunters searching for wolves came upon three deer, a doe, and two half-grown fawns. Their hounds gave chase and nearly caught up with the deer when they reached rough country. Here the deer broke into their famous leaping, soaring bounds that car-ried them as if on wings from ridge to ridge. The hounds, who had to run up and down the hills, were soon winded and gave up the chase. The agile deer escaped.

On another occasion, Mr. Seton measured the distances between tracks of a bounding blacktail deer. He discovered that these amazing creatures sprang fifteen to twenty-five feet in each graceful leap.

The aspen grove shimmers in the sunlight. Each straight white-barked trunk bears branches of pale green, feather-light leaves which turn and dance in the breeze. Because of their constantly moving leaves, the early settlers called these trees quaking aspens.

Among the aspen trees stand many stumps, twelve to eighteen inches high. Each has a pointed tip. This is the logging ground of the beaver colony. Trees cut from the grove were used to dam the stream. Others were stored under the water so that the beavers could have bark for winter food.

Now the beavers have left the meadow for their seasonal visit to other beaver colonies.

In the aspen grove, a tangle of fallen limbs makes a favorite playground and hiding place for chipmunks, ground squirrels, mice, and weasels. So it is that the work of the beavers improves the *habitat,* or home, for many other meadow creatures.

Now, in late spring, the meadow is carpeted with a thick coat of waving grass. Here, many kinds of grasses grow together, mixed with broad-leaved plants. But the grasses predominate. Common among these are blue grass and tufted hair grass. Near the creek and around the beaver pond, coarse grasslike sedges grow.

Grass is food for many animals, large and small. Deer and bears feed partly on grass. Some birds eat it. Mice eat tender grass shoots, and later its seed furnish their winter fare. Pocket gophers live on roots and grass.

Many of the birds use grass to build nests. The meadow mice make winter huts of dried grass, while many of the small burrowing animals line their nesting hollows with grass. Grass makes a meadow. The dictionary definition of meadow is "A grassy open space."

Early flowers are gone. Their seed heads wave green and brown among the grasses. But in drier spots away from the stream, glow the yellow-orange daisies called balsam root. These spicy-sweet blossoms with arrow-shaped, gray-green leaves are among the gayest of summer flowers in the high meadows of western North America.

Out of his hiding place beneath a fallen tree, scutters a furry mouse. Above his brownish-gray back two huge ears stand up stiffly. He turns to stare down his tunnel through the grass stems, his round black eyes alert and watchful. Something moves. The stems quiver. The mouse freezes, then whirls and darts back to his shelter.

Oiling his way through the grass, glides a yellow-striped garter snake. The deadly enemy of most of the small meadow animals stretches himself out on the mouse road and waits. The next mouse who tries to use this highway will be sorry.

The wary mice do most of their traveling at night. This snake is not likely to catch any today.

Finally the snake slithers on toward the creek. There,

Beaked sedge, a common plant in wet places.

near a damp backwater puddle, he catches some slugs. With his stomach full, the lazy reptile curls himself on a flat rock and goes to sleep in the sun.

Into the meadow waddles the female bear. She stands high, nose up, sniffing, peering. Her cubs follow, rising up beside their mother. Then the bear family walks slowly toward the stream.

That flat rock in the sun beckons mother bear. It is just what she needs. Stealthily the huge furry beast creeps forward, growls, and grabs with her powerful paw. The garter snake squirms in the bear's grasp. This is one bit of dinner she hadn't planned. The cubs join their mother to share the snake. Then the big bear settles down on the rock. The cubs lie in the grass behind her.

Lying very flat, with her chin hanging over the stream, the mother bear dangles her right front foot into the water. She growls softly, warning the cubs to be quiet. Not a hair moves. The big bear waits.

With a splash the bear jerks her dangling paw from the creek. A shining trout lands on the bank. Mother and cubs pounce. They eat the fish, then wander on down the meadow, stopping to crop some tender grass shoots.

Then, on a smooth place halfway between the stream and the forest, the mother bear stops. She sits down in the grass, the cubs beside her. They wait. The old bear darts forward. In her sharp claws she holds a limp ground squirrel. One blow from her powerful paw has broken its back. Once more the bears eat. With satisfied grunts they waddle toward the forest, stopping to turn a flat stone and lick a few insects from the damp soil.

Ground squirrels make vast networks of tunnels in the earth. They watch for enemies close by the mounded entrances to their burrows.

The ground squirrel colony panics. A chattering danger message echoes through their network of tunnels.

One old male, his cheek pouches bulging with food, scampers into a nest tunnel to spread the sad news. Perhaps he tells the five young ones in the burrow all about the bear menace.

Gold and black swallowtail butterflies on a mallow plant.

Minutes pass, then an inquisitive nose pokes up from a tunnel opening. Bright eyes look around for dark bear shadows. The ground squirrel sniffs the air for bear smell. Then he comes out and looks again. With a chirp and a flick of his furry tail he scampers down the trail. Soon other squirrels follow. The grass bustles with ground squirrel business.

Ground squirrels make vast networks of tunnels in the earth. They loosen the soil so that the roots of plants can more easily penetrate it. Because they are there, the grass and other meadow plants grow more luxuriantly, for the ground squirrels and their digging and burrowing cousins are cultivators of the meadow soil.

Hovering, darting on painted wings, butterflies dance above the meadow grass. Around the lavender blossoms of the mallows, brown and black checkered skippers gather. They settle on the flowers to uncoil long spiraled tubes, or *proboscises*, which they push deep into the blossoms to suck nectar.

The swallowtails, with long, pointed lower wings sail over the grass, golden bright as yellow mustard flowers.

Yellow butterflies with black dotted wings, tiny coppery-tinted elfins and the delicate blue butterflies flutter over the wild vetch and other *legumes*, plants of the pea and bean family.

The butterflies of our meadow hatched from eggs and pupas when the weather grew warm in spring. Now, in summer, they are busy preparing for the next generation. Each female butterfly lays her eggs in a secluded place, often as a small colony, or patch, on the underside of a leaf or twig. These eggs are then fertilized by the male butterfly and covered with a hard, scale-like shell.

The eggs hatch into *caterpillars,* sometimes fuzzy, sometimes covered with shiny, scaly sheaths. Often the caterpillars have coloring that resembles their butterfly parents. They spend their lives eating and growing. When a caterpillar's body grows too big for his skin, he sheds his old covering and a new one develops in its place. Sometimes a caterpillar will go through four or five of these *molts,* or skin sheddings, before he grows into his adult size.

After the caterpillar eats enough to attain his full size, he goes into another stage known as the *pupa.* He spins a *cocoon,* or casing, around himself and attaches this to the underside of a twig or leaf with a thread of spun silk. There the pupa swings, quietly changing into a butterfly.

Some caterpillars hatch from eggs in late summer and hibernate through the winter, emerging in spring as butterflies. These hibernating species cover the pupa with a hard casing that protects it from cold and wet weather.

Other kinds of butterflies lay their eggs in late summer or autumn, sometimes in holes in the ground, sometimes protected by scaly covers. Then, when spring comes, the eggs hatch into caterpillars and the life cycle of the butterflies begins anew.

Butterflies die at the end of summer, for their fragile bodies cannot withstand the rigors of cold weather. The race lives on in the next generation of hibernated pupas or protected eggs.

Caterpillars are plant eaters. They consume leaves and new grass shoots, each kind preferring a different plant. Some varieties of caterpillars live on pine trees and eat parts of the needles. Many trees are damaged by these small wormlike insects with the voracious appetites.

The caterpillar of one variety of moth, a night-flying cousin of the butterfly called the needleminer, attacks pine trees. In Yosemite National Park in California, these caterpillars have, during some seasons, completely destroyed the needles on lodgepole pine trees. Th trees stand bare, "ghost forests."

The meadow grass stirs with brown and tan grasshoppers. These are fully-grown insects. Soon it will be time to begin the mating and egg-laying ritual that will carry the species into the season ahead.

The small male grasshoppers fly into the air in a mating dance, then settle to join the females on a gravelly spot near the creek. There, closely surrounded by males, the big sturdy females lay their eggs, depositing them into the gravel bed to protect them from birds and the weather.

Each female grasshopper lays twenty to fifty tiny yellowish eggs, resembling minute bananas. She places these eggs in the gravel with her special *ovipositor*, then secrets a sticky fluid with which she covers the eggs. This sticky cover hardens into a shell-like pod. As it hardens, tiny bits of sand and gravel adhere to its gluey sides. Thus, the finished pod looks like the gravel which surrounds and protects it, making it very difficult to find.

All winter long, the eggs lie under the gravel in a dormant or sleeping state. When spring warms the

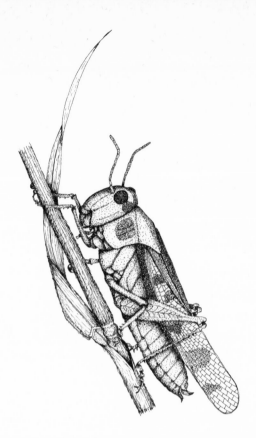

A large female clear-winged grasshopper. This western mountain grasshopper is one of the commonest of the grasshopper family. Females are larger and thicker than the males.

meadow, the eggs stir. By late spring, tiny pale wormlike *larvae* break out of their cages and wriggle themselves to the surface of the gravel bed. Almost immediately they shed their first skins to become *nymphs*, tiny partly-formed grasshoppers, pale yellow or greenish yellow.

A flightless nymph sheds his skin five times. As he eats green leaves and grows, his body becomes too large for his skin. The old skin splits and the immature grasshopper emerges, larger and with a new covering. His body, too, changes. Slowly his wings develop. At last the grass-hopper flies.

Then the cycle of mating, egg laying, winter dormancy, spring hatching, growing, shedding skins, and growing larger, begins all over again. The species lives through the winter only in the eggs hidden deep in the gravel bed, for all adult grasshoppers die when cold weather comes.

Most every plant, animal, and insect of the meadow helps furnish food for another species or kind of creature. So it is with the butterflies and grasshoppers. In the worm or caterpillar stage, both moths and butterflies are eaten in large numbers by birds. Grasshopper eggs and nymphs furnish many a meal for small birds, while the adult insects fall prey to skunks, bears, and large birds.

If it weren't for insect-eating birds, the population of insects would increase so that shrubs, trees, and grass might be totally destroyed. Because the birds keep the insect population balanced, there are seldom too many for their food supply.

Life in the meadow, and indeed in all of nature, is a chain of eating and being eaten.

As the summer day draws to a close, a tawny, spotted, female bobcat pads softly into the open between the trees. She stations herself behind the rock pile at the side of the beaver pond and watches. The cat crouches, quiet, watchful, her black-tipped ears blending with the colors of the stones.

Under this rock pile two marmots, or rockchucks, have their home. Their deep safe burrow begins just beside the last outcropping and extends downward at a slant. Most of this home is under the rocks. But the opening, with its mound of dirt, is a perfect place from which to watch meadow life. The marmots are content with green grass and clover to eat in summer, and a warm dry place to sleep through the winter cold.

On this still, late afternoon, the male marmot awakes from a short nap in the darkness of his burrow. He decides to take one last look around before dark. Sleepily he edges up his tunnel. He pokes his dark nose outside, sees no enemy, then scrambles to the dirt mound at the burrow entrance.

Quicker than sight, the bobcat pounces. With one blow of her big powerful paw, she kills the unwary marmot. One foot on her prey, the cat looks around the meadow.

A squawking jay swoops overhead. The bobtailed cat growls.

Like silent shadows, two smaller bobcats emerge from the underbrush. They trot toward the waiting huntress to share the family supper.

Together the three bobcats devour the marmot. With bloody paws and faces, they climb to the top of the rock pile. Licking their paws, they wash away every trace of their feast. Then, purring loudly, the cats rest awhile on the sunny rocks. Satisfied, they disappear below the beaver dam.

The marmot ate the grass and clover in the meadow. Then the bobcat ate the marmot. The bobcats will, in their time, die, too. Then the flesh of the dead cats will be broken

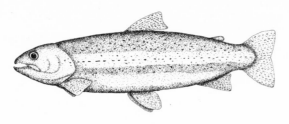

RAINBOW TROUT

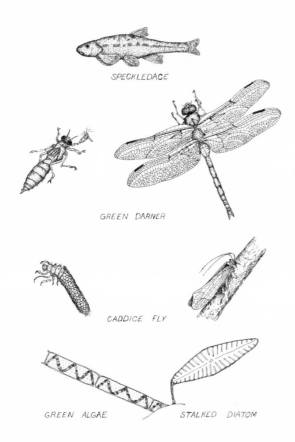

SPECKLEDACE

GREEN DARNER

CADDICE FLY

GREEN ALGAE   STALKED DIATOM

A food chain in the stream: The simple plants, called algae, shown in the lower diagram, cling to the rocks in the stream. On these feed the caddis fly larvae, left; and adult, right. The green darner dragonfly nymph, left; and adult, right, eat the caddis flies. The speckledace, or minnow, eats dragonfly nymphs and caddis flies. The rainbow trout at the top of the page eats the speckledace, the green darner, and the caddis fly.

down, eaten, by *bacteria* and *protozoa*, microscopic organisms which return it to the soil. Then this soil will furnish nutrients so that more plants may grow. These plants, with carbon dioxide and water, will make more green food through the process of photosynthesis. Thus the *food chain,* or cycle, continues to sustain life on earth.

Many different food chains interlock throughout all of nature. Together they are called a *food web.*

Tall firs on the west side of the meadow shadow the grass with light and dark. Moving slowly, a furry animal comes from the direction of the aspen grove. He waddles around the beaver pond and stops beside the creek. The night-roaming raccoon has awakened from his daylight sleep in a fallen log. He reaches down at the edge of the stream and grabs a small frog. The frog squirms, but the raccoon crushes him against the pebbly creekside. Then he reaches down into the water and carefully washes his prey.

Before the raccoon eats, he raises his masked face to look around him. Satisfied that all is safe, he settles down to his meal. Soon another raccoon appears, hunting frogs and insects, or an occasional mussel along the stream.

Raccoons live in most of our states. Unusual coloring makes this small relative of the bear easy to identify. The raccoon, or coon, has a black-masked face, yellow-brown or grayish fur that is black-tipped on his back and very light underneath. His bushy tail is ringed with black and light tan, or gray stripes.

Night is the favorite hunting time for raccoons. They prowl the woods and meadows, always near water, hunt-

The raccoons live in hollow trees or logs.

ing for anything that can possibly be used for food. Like bears, they like food left out by campers. They are omnivorous, eating flesh, fruit, or vegetables.

During the winter, raccoons hibernate for short periods. Where winters are very long, they may sleep four or five months. But they sleep lightly and often awake and come out of their hollow trees with the slightest warming of the weather. Where winters are short, raccoons may not sleep at all.

The two raccoons walk up the creek bank, turning small stones to get insects hiding under them, dabbling in the water for crayfish or mussels. So they will spend the night, until dawn sends them back to sleep in a hollow tree or log.

A full moon sails in the cloudless summer sky. A coyote calls, then another joins in. A cool breeze ruffles the grass as the creatures of the night claim the meadow for their own.

The yellow-orange flowers of balsam root glow in the sun.

❧ 5

The Meadow Suns Itself

Midsummer sun glitters the meadow with early light. Birds twitter morning songs, more softly now with the advancing season. From a nest in the fir tree two jays sail out to find insects for their hungry half-grown chicks.

On padded paws, a coyote slinks from the aspen grove. He pauses by the beaver pond, then continues warily on to the rock pile. He sniffs, turning round and round. Marmot smell is strong, but the remaining marmot is sleeping below the rocks.

Chipmunks were there, too, but they heard the enemy coming and dived into their burrows. The coyote scratches the earth, then trots away. Down to the creek he goes, sniffing, looking. He drinks.

The coyote raises his gray-brown head. Big ears point forward. He watches, one front foot raised, black-tipped bushy tail switching from side to side. Suddenly he bounds forward and begins to dig, throwing the soft soil behind him in a cloud. Down into the earth pokes his nose. The coyote brings up a limp pocket gopher. With one crunch of tiny bones, the hunter swallows the rodent. He trots on. Before this day and night have gone, our coyote and his mate will kill and eat several mice, gophers, ground squirrels, and perhaps a rabbit.

Coyotes help keep the natural balance in the meadow. If they did not raid the gopher and mouse colonies, these small creatures would increase rapidly. Too many of them would greatly decrease the supply of seeds, roots, and plants available for each. Many would die of starvation.

If the small animals were to become so numerous that they ate all the food in the meadow—seeds, roots, everything—there would be nothing to start new plants. When animals increase beyond their food supplies, they greatly damage or even completely destroy the sources of those supplies.

Losing all plant cover from the meadow would leave the soil unprotected. *Erosion,* or wearing away by wind and water, could soon turn the meadow surface into bare earth, fit for neither plants nor animals.

So it is that the coyote benefits all meadow life by catching smaller animals. He provides food for himself and helps keep a balance of animals and plants, which aids the continuing cycle.

The large coyote of our meadow lives in high elevations in North America. Commonly called the mountain coyote, he is much like his slightly smaller prairie-wolf cousin. Mountain coyotes often have thick fur coats, while the plains-dwelling coyotes have thin scraggly fur.

For centuries, stories of the cunning and wisdom of

Coyotes mate for life, sharing everything.

the coyote were told by people of the Americas. The ancient lore of the Aztecs of Mexico built many legends around a coyote god. From his Aztec name, *Coyotl*, comes our name for him.

Among Indian people of North America, stories of the coyote are common, told to the children to explain beginnings. According to the folklore of the Nez Percé Indians of northern Idaho, and their cousins the Yakimas and Umatillas of Washington and Oregon, Itsayaya, the coyote, was a powerful ruler, king of the world before man came. With cleverness, knowledge, and sometimes by trickery, this coyote king presided over an empire of animals.

Hunters and trappers tell many true stories of coyote wisdom. Dr. W. T. Hornaday told of watching a coyote in

Montana. The naturalist wanted this particular animal for a specimen. Each time Dr. Hornaday rode from camp with his rifle across his saddle, the coyote watched him, just out of gunshot range. But when the scientist rode out unarmed, the coyote sat down in the middle of the trail and would not move to let the horse and rider pass. Surely that coyote was wise beyond our imagining.

Coyotes are known for their voices. At evening the coyotes gather, perhaps four or five together. They select a high place—a hill or knoll. Then, facing each other in a circle, noses close together, they lift their heads and sing. Throughout the western part of North America, the yipping, barking wail of the coyote shatters the night stillness. These sociable animals seem to delight in the noises they make. Some people think the coyote song is sad, but its seems more likely that they sing for the joy of living. Maybe they celebrate good hunting and full stomachs.

Coyotes mate for life. They share everything; hunting, caring for the young, selecting and improving the den where they live. Only when the two to six pups are very tiny, does the male coyote hunt without his mate. Then he goes alone and brings his kill to the den where he divides his food with the female. Later, when the pups can be left for short times, both parents hunt and bring their meat home to share with their young.

These gray-brown dwellers in forest and meadow owe much of their hunting skill to their speed. In short dashes, fifty yards or less, coyotes can outrun most other animals. The young of many larger animals fall victim to these cunning hunters.

After our meadow coyote eats the pocket gopher, he disappears among the trees. But the gophers panic. In their colony of underground tunnels and heaped hills of fresh dirt, there is a squeaking and scurrying deeper into the protecting earth.

Pocket gophers spend most of their lives underground. These sturdy diggers make many-branched tunnels. Their living quarters are hollowed-out places lined with dried, shredded grass. The shiny, brown, four-inch-long animals come out only occasionally to eat grass, usually very near their burrow entrances. They stuff extra food into huge

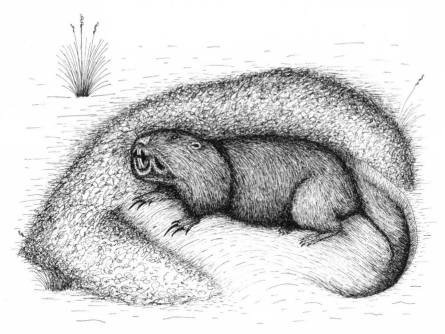

As the pocket gopher digs with his long-clawed, short front legs, he pushes soil to the surface with his chest and front feet. His four sharp front teeth grow outside his furry lips. Beside his mouth on each cheek is an open fur-lined pouch.

pockets or cheek pouches and store it away in their burrows for use during times of famine.

Gophers live over most of the meadow. Our meadow
is dotted with the mounds and hills of the pocket gophers,
fan-shaped piles of earth.

As a gopher digs his tunnel, he pushes the extra soil
up to the surface with his front feet and chest. Then he
backs down his tunnel, or turns around and runs down it.
As he digs, he finds succulent roots which he eats, or carries away to store in his burrow. By far the largest part of
this digger's diet is roots.

The gopher pokes his nose from his hole, and with
his razor-sharp front teeth crops the grass around his burrow entrance. These teeth, two above and two below, grow
outside his furry lips.

A gopher may sometimes journey a few feet away
from home for some extra-fine forage. He stuffs his pouches
and scampers back. In the plant materials the gopher carries underground are seeds of grasses and other plants.
Some of these drop and take root. Thus the pocket gopher
distributes plants around the meadow.

As the gopher digs with his long front claws and
pushes his earth loads to the surface, he cultivates the
meadow soil. This loose, stirred soil is ideal for growing
grass and plants of all kinds. So in his small underground
way, the tiny pocket gopher helps to preserve the meadow.

Along the creek, summer plants bloom. Raising their
tall, lacy heads high above the grass, cow parsnips nod in
the sun.

A sound of cracking sticks echoes from below the

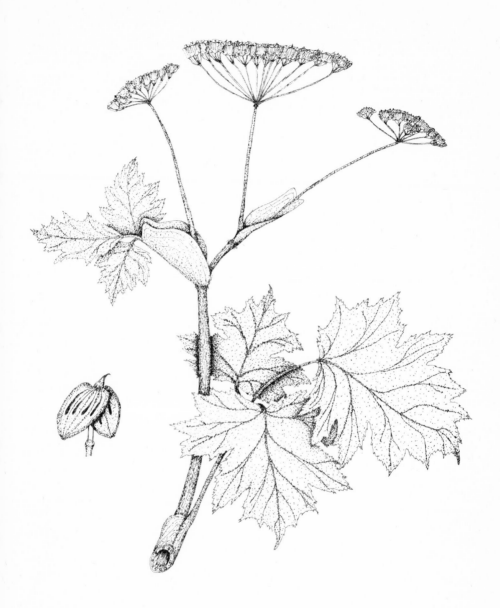

Cow parsnips raise their lacy heads above the grass.

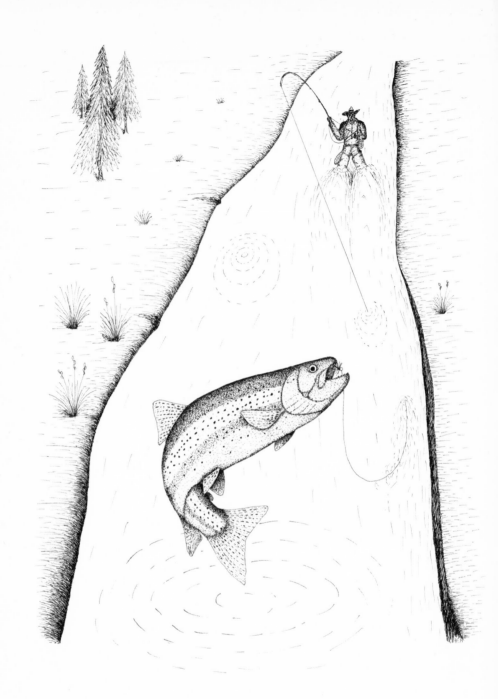

The shining trout leaps into the air.

beaver pond. Up from the valley tramps a fisherman. He skirts the pond and walks along the creek. Into the deep pool below the shallow rapids, he casts his fishing line. Out of the depths a ten-inch rainbow trout rises and grabs the fly. Line taut, the man reels in his catch. Fighting for his life, the shining fish leaps into the air. But the match is unequal. What small fish can hope to win against the strength of a man?

The fisherman stuffs the dead trout into his creel and goes on up the creek and out of the meadow. Where the fish darted to terrorize minnows and water insects, peace reigns. Now the other inhabitants of the pool can multiply and grow without disturbance, until another trout swims up the creek to live in the pool below the rapids.

Up the creek from the beaver pond, something moves in the grass. A fluffy brush of black and white fur waves slowly back and forth. There, hunting for insects, is a skunk. But look. This is a whole family of skunks. Four youngsters follow in a straight line behind their mother.

The skunks are hunting. Mother skunk pounces on a grasshopper. Then she turns a stone with her front paw and catches insects which hide beneath it. The young imitate the mother, grabbing awkwardly at beetles which scurry away into the grass.

Skunks are slow-moving, but they have no need for speed. Every animal of the woods and meadow respects the skunk and gives him a wide berth. For skunks are armed with powerful weapons, bags full of putrid scent which they squirt from special openings under their tails when they are molested or alarmed.

Hunting insects for her family, the mother skunk turns a stone with her front paw.

Any creature foolhardy enough to annoy a beautiful black and white striped skunk can expect to be sprayed with his blinding, stinking scent.

Skunk families travel together until the young are nearly grown. Now, in summer, the baby skunks are half-grown, exact copies of their furry black and white mother, beautiful but dangerous.

From the trout pool below the rapids, the creek flows slowly until it reaches the quiet beaver pond. Here is another world, the world of water and all the plants and animals which live in it and upon it.

Some of the living organisms in the pond are so tiny that they cannot be seen without the aid of a very powerful miscroscope.

Water has more of the essentials for life than any other environment. Because of this, the variety of living bodies in a pond is almost uncountable.

Most numerous of the pond creatures are the *plankton*. These are very tiny bodies which reproduce rapidly, especially on warm summer days. Some of them are green with a minute drop of green-plant chlorophyll. Still others are microscopic animals. Oxygen is essential to plankton. Some of them breathe the oxygen dissolved in the water by the action of wind on the surface of the pond. Still others float on the top where they breathe directly from the air.

Plankton furnish food for water insects, and these, in turn, nourish fish and frogs. Here in the pond, as on the land, a food chain operates, one kind of plant or animal depending upon another in order to live.

Around the edges of the pond grow many kinds of plants. In their shelter live frogs, snails, beetles, water skippers, and dragonflies.

Now, in summer, a family of mallard ducks swims on the pond. They especially like the marshy edges, where they upend to feed on bottom-dwelling plants or to catch insects hiding in the rushes.

Midday summer stillness spreads its calm over the meadow. Creatures rest in their cool burrows or in the shade of the forest trees.

When the sun stands overhead, the quiet is broken by the sound of a motor. Up the track from the lower country chugs a camper truck. It stops beside the benches and fireplace and out tumble three boys and a girl. After them come their parents. The meadow echoes with shouts and laughter. The children run everywhere, gathering wood for a campfire, chasing butterflies and ground squirrels.

Together the people pitch a tent and take food supplies from their car. A campfire crackles. The smell of frying bacon drifts across the meadow.

As the day progresses toward evening, the children explore the whole meadow, running after chipmunks, terrifying the small animals in the grass.

Pocket gophers burrow deeper into the earth. Even so, they do not completely escape the pounding of heavy feet that caves in their carefully-made tunnels. In one spot, a whole nest is flattened when a boy jumps on the soft soil above it.

Mice scurry into hiding to avoid running feet. Even

if the mice escape with their lives, their homes are damaged. Their food supply of grass and seeds lies crushed underfoot.

At dusk a group of deer appears at the upper end of the meadow. Two does with fawns stand alert, ears forward, sniffing the strange smell of campfire and cooking. Then they quietly fade back into the forest.

A few minutes later, a huge buck with spreading antlers moves out of the sheltering woods. He surveys the camp, alert to danger. Snorting his disdain, he disappears among the trees.

Night darkens the meadow. Around the glowing fire the campers sit, happy in their retreat. They do not know that, because they came, countless small creatures have less to eat. Unaware of disturbing meadow life, the family enjoys the peace of the mountains.

The people crawl into their sleeping bags. Only the night creatures, the owls and a distant howling coyote, disturb the stillness.

Up the creek waddles a dark figure. He walks, flat-footed and sure, to the camp. There, on the picnic table, the bear smells something more delicious than anything that grows in the woods or meadow. He must find out what it is. Rising onto his hind legs, he reaches toward that smell. But, alas, he touches only a wooden box.

With one strong paw, the black bear pulls the box toward him. The smell excites him to frenzy. He must get it. He must. He claws at the box. Bang! It falls from the table and bursts open. The bear tears at the spilled food, searching for that tantalizing smell. He finds it—bacon.

With a shout and a blinding flash of light, the angry man bursts from the tent. "Thief!" he shouts. "Get out of here!"

Frightened and confused, the bear runs, clutching the package of bacon in his teeth.

The campers pick up the remains of their food supplies and lock them in their car, then go back to bed.

As peace returns to the meadow, a golden animal slips from the underbrush. The mountain lion, or cougar, is on his way to the creek for a drink. But the camp lies across his path.

Staring with wary green eyes, the big cat stops and switches his long tail from side to side. Who has dared to block his path to the creek? The cougar retreats, then emerges farther up the meadow. He will have to go around that clump of willows to get water. No matter. He trots on, then stops beside the willows, sniffing, looking. He leaps. A long desperate squeal pierces the quiet as a cotton-tail rabbit dies under the sharp claws of the giant golden cat.

Because the campers had blocked his usual path to water, the mountain lion found and killed the rabbit. Thus the chain of cause and effect goes on. Now there will be one less rabbit to gnaw the willows when winter comes.

Peace returns to the meadow, but only for a while. High in the half-dead pine, the great horned owl shouts, "Whoo-whoo, whoo-whooo?" To the night creatures he says, "I'm here, whooo's next?" Then he swoops on silent wings out of his tree and over the grassy spaces.

By the creek, yarrows bloom white in the sun.

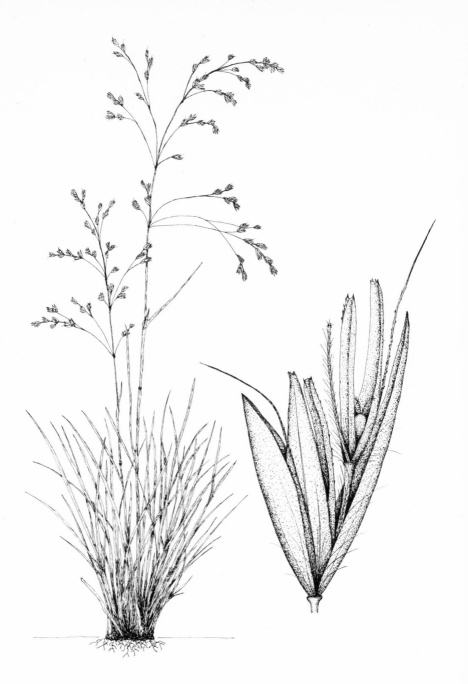

Tufted hairgrass with a full seed head. One enlarged spikelet with two seeds, or florets, is at the right.

6

The Meadow Parches

Summer grows old in the meadow. Sun-browned grass nods fully matured seed heads. Beside the creek and the beaver pond, grass and sedges grow tall and green. But the stream runs in only a trickle. A shrunken pond exposes its muddy margins to the drying sun.

At the edge of the meadow, high in a tall fir, a red squirrel greets the dawn, chattering a warning: "Don't come near. This is mine." Bits of green hull shatter down. Then a whole pinecone tumbles to the needle-covered earth with a dull thump. The squirrel runs down the tree almost as fast as the cone falls. He leaps upon his prize, scolding. Tearing at the hulls, the chickaree stuffs the unripe nuts into his cheeks. He rushes to store them.

Chipmunks work during early morning hours. They fill their cheeks with grass seeds and carry them away to underground caches.

Up the trail from the valley below, drifts the sound of a motor. A car, loaded high with camping gear, bumps

High in a tall fir tree, a red squirrel greets the dawn.

The jay squawks a warning.

over the gopher-hillocked track and stops at the fireplace beside the creek. A man, a woman, and a boy get out of the car. They unload camping equipment and pitch a tent.

Soon cooking smells drift on the lazy summer air. The campers eat, laughing as they rush to finish.

"Hurry, Dad," urges the boy. "Hurry, before it rains."

"Storm up there, all right." The man stands and looks toward the mountain where a dark cloud covers the peak.

"We'll clean up later," says the woman. "Let's get some trout for supper."

The three people take their fishing gear and start upstream to harass the shining trout.

When they are halfway to the upper end of the meadow, a jay flies squawking overhead. Another joins him. Chipmunks set up a chatter. The squirrels scold. Suddenly the meadow rings with alarm.

A sharp wind blows down the mountain.

The fishermen glance back toward the camp.

"Fire!" shouts the woman. "Run!"

They run back to the camp.

"Our fire! We forgot our fire," sobs the boy.

The dry grass roars. Angry flames lick out to spread the fire. One side of the meadow blazes and crackles.

The people grab buckets and scoop water from the creek, flinging it over their car and tent, fighting the roaring flames. The fire burns one corner of the tent. Flying embers leave many charred holes in the canvas.

The small creatures who live on the meadow floor are not so fortunate. They have little defense against the killer, fire. Gophers and moles burrow into the earth, digging frantically to get below the heat. But the meadow mice do not escape so easily. Their burrows are shallow. Many of them, out looking for food, burn to death almost before they know the fire is coming.

Insects, too, are engulfed by the fire. Hopping, flying, crawling, they hurry away from the heat, but the tongues of flame lick out hungrily with voracious speed. Many die in the path of the fire. Some insects get away from the flames. Others hide under stones or logs and escape.

Black smoke billows up as the fire roars on. It nears the trees at the edge of the meadow. A towering pine ignites and blazes. Another burns, and another, as the flames rush forward.

Suddenly the wind changes, sending the wall of flame

back upon itself. Lightning crackles. Thunder drums its way down the mountain and across the meadow. Then comes rain, a few enormous scattered drops. Faster and faster it falls until a wall of water washes the land.

The fire smolders, then steams, and sputters out. The creek roars, swollen suddenly with rainwater. Muddy, choked with fire-blackened debris, the creek dumps its load into the beaver pond.

The fire slowly abated, but left its scars on the land. On the east side of the stream nearly half of the meadow floor lies dead and black, the plants a sooty, brittle stubble.

Fire destroys, but also stimulates new growth. It removes a tangle of old roots and stems and returns their minerals to the soil in the form of ash. For the rest of this season, there will be little growth where the fire has burned. The fire-blackened grass and scorched bushes will remain for a while as reminders that campers were careless. Almost immediately, the brushy plants will begin to sprout from the roots.

Next spring, after the heavy winter snows and early rains, green grass and flowers will cover the burn scar. Fire seldom destroys all seeds, so there are enough to start growth again when weather conditions are right.

The fire killed deer brush, but only the tops of the willows, alders, and chokecherries. Small forest trees scattered near the edge of the meadow were completely destroyed.

Without fire, these trees would, after many years, turn the meadow into a forest. Now, with shrubs and trees burned, the meadow grasses and flowers can grow. Fire helps keep the space open, helps maintain the meadow as it is.

Fireweed, with its tall red-purple blooms, is often the first plant to cover burn scars in the forest. Its seeds need fire to stimulate growth. Sometimes great burned areas are covered the following season with glowing fields of fireweed. The minerals released by the fire stimulate the growth of this and many other plants, so that the burned area produces more than the usual amount of plant growth.

Where the forest edge burned, fireweed will grow next spring, followed in later seasons by grasses and flowers. Then brush will invade the grassland, and, finally, the area of burned trees will return again to forest.

On the old meadow floor, some new plants, annual grasses, and flowers will appear. Within one or two seasons the meadow will return to its original state. Catastrophes such as fire stimulate nature to repair the damage.

Many mice, and insects, as well as some ground squirrels and pocket gophers lost their lives in the fire. Other creatures will find less to eat because seeds and grass were destroyed by the flames. Some small meadow dwellers may starve during the coming winter.

After the ashes cool, a weasel comes from the forest edge. He stops at the blackened ground, sniffs the air, and runs back and forth. He lifts his brown-capped head, waving it from side to side. Then, stepping daintily on white feet, he loops his way to the upper end of the burn and out into the grass.

The weasel runs down a path tramped in the tall stems

by white-footed mice. His slender body slips easily along the mouse road. He comes to a burrow entrance, sniffs, then slides down into it.

Soon, pattering swiftly, comes a mouse. The weasel lies very still. Into his burrow ducks the mouse. The weasel grabs him by the throat. The mouse had no chance against this smallest and perhaps cruelest of the carnivores.

The weasel of our meadow is the short-tailed, or lesser, weasel. With a small, pointed head, a slender body

The crafty weasel grabs the homecoming mouse.

only six inches long, and a tail about one and one-fourth inches long, he is small enough to follow the mice into their burrows. Since he lives almost entirely upon mice, mouse-eater weasel is another common name for him.

But fire destroyed many of the mice and the food supply for others. What will happen to the weasels without mice to eat?

Survival of all the animals of the meadow depends upon their food supplies. The weakest starve or are eaten by other animals. So when there are fewer mice in the meadow, some members of the weasel clan will starve. Then, with fewer weasels, more of the remaining mice will survive to reproduce and build the mouse population again. This, of course, will depend on the food available to the mice. Nature is constantly at work to keep the food in balance with the animals who need it to live.

When food supplies are scarce, only the strongest animals survive. Those carnivores who cannot hunt as skillfully as their neighbors do not catch enough to keep going and hence starve to death. So it is with the prey of the carnivores. The weak and lagging deer falls to the hunting mountain lion. Coyotes easily catch and kill a limping rabbit. When grass is scarce, the grasseaters starve. First to go are always the weakest, those less able to go long distances for food, or who were weakened by disease or injury before food became scarce.

When fire, or some other disaster, destroys the food supply, only the animals who are strong enough to leave the fire-damaged area can hope to survive.

Among the animals, it is always the strongest, the

cleverest, the fleetest of foot, who survive. These are the pick of the species, those best adapted to life in the woods and meadows. They will reproduce, passing their strong characteristics to their offspring. This rule of nature is called *survival of the fittest.*

Dusk shadows the meadow. Into the clearing opposite the burn come three deer, a doe, and two half-grown fawns. They drink from the creek, then nibble at the willows. The fawns run in circles, bucking and kicking.

Farther up toward the mountain, an antlered buck slips out from the shadow of the trees. He watches the frolicking fawns, head high, proud. Then the buck moves slowly to the creek's edge. He drinks, eats from a clump of deer brush, then disappears silently into the forest.

Up from the beaver dam, a mountain lion glides. He hides behind the rock pile and watches the deer.

One fawn runs far from the other deer. He hides in the bushes, then leaps out suddenly. He is small, not as agile as his brother.

The big cat watches, green eyes aglitter.

The fawn dances down to the creek opposite the rock pile, then turns and scampers back to his mother.

From his hiding place creeps the cougar, slowly, silently. The doe raises her head, sniffs the air. She snorts. The careful fawn stays close to her side, but the foolish one darts back to the creek.

With a silent leap the big cat clears the dividing creek. The foolish fawn falls, struggles, then lies quiet. With a low growl, the mountain lion tears at the flesh of his victim.

The doe snorts wildly. Trembling, the remaining fawn follows her into the forest.

Overhead, two mallard ducks, a male and a female, circle the beaver pond. With a whirr of wings they glide onto the water, spraying a fountain on either side. Smoothly they sail across the pond, then paddle toward the rushes. Three young ducks swim out to meet them. Quacking and chattering, they disappear among the thick stems.

Darkness blankets the meadow. A night hawk zooms his hunting song as he swoops and darts low to catch night-flying insects.

Away on a distant hill a coyote serenades the night.

7

The Meadow Prepares

Morning drifts cool and crisp over the meadow. Through the brown grass the leaves of wild geraniums glow scarlet. The sun glints on the black burn scar. Down near the lower end of the beaver pond, the aspens shake their trembling golden robes. For it is autumn. Frost has touched the meadow with a brush dipped crimson, yellow, brown—a final glowing salute to the fading days of summer.

The waters of the beaver pond ripple in the breeze, shaking the painted shadows of the forest trees.

Into the meadow clatters the ranger's truck. Mark Stevens and Jim Marshall climb out.

"Seems only yesterday we put up the table, Jim. The summer has gone very fast." Mark looks up and down the meadow. "That was quite a fire. What luck that storm came up."

"Could have been much worse." Jim looks far up the meadow. "Look, Mark, over there." Jim points across the creek to where three deer browse around a shrub.

"That big fellow is a beauty. Look at those antlers! Hope he escapes the hunters."

Together the men load the table onto the truck. Then they tramp to the upper end of the meadow and straighten the bright orange snow-survey sign on a tree.

"These signs won't stay put. Maybe that big bear rubs on them," says Jim, as he hammers in new nails.

"We'll fix the one at the lower end as.we leave so we can keep to a straight line when we take our snow readings this winter." Mark adjusts the sign. Then the two men return to the truck and clatter off down the track.

As the morning sun warms the meadow, animals begin to work and sing. Everywhere, except in the burned place, chipmunks run, dart, scold, and chatter. Their cheek pouches bulge with seeds. Chipmunks build underground granaries and fill them with seeds of grasses, pine nuts, and dried berries. Almost any seed will do, but their favorites are the grass seeds, the wild grain of the meadow.

One chipmunk, captured in autumn in a California meadow, had over one thousand grass seeds stuffed into his bulging pouches.

A huge chipmunk hurries back and forth from a thick clump of grass to the base of a stump. He ducks into a hole, then pops out again to go for another cheek-load of seeds. He runs to the grass, picks up the fallen seeds, and begins to stuff his pouches. With agile, handlike front feet, the chipmunk stuffs a few seeds first into one pouch, then into the other, balancing his load. When each cheek bulges so that his head looks much too large for his body, the busy little animal scampers back to his hole.

One chipmunk had over one thousand tiny grass seeds stuffed into his bulging pouches. In spite of his load he tried to scold.

The chipmunks will not open their granaries until spring. They curl up in their burrows and hibernate. With the first warm spring days, chipmunks come out. It is then that they eat their stored food. Each chipmunk works very hard to store enough, or more than enough, to last until seed time the following season.

The fat marmot suns on her rock pile.

This year, because fire destroyed many seeds, they must hunt for every one they carry into their burrows.

Competing with the chipmunks, and sometimes quarreling with them over choice seeds, are the ground squirrels. They too, store food in their tunnels, but are less dependent on stored supplies than their chipmunk cousins. Ground squirrels eat grass and bulbs and can live on these in the spring until seeds come again.

The red squirrels, or chickarees, bustle in the trees at the meadow's edge. They cut cones and shell out the nuts. The squirrels carry the nuts out onto the meadow floor and bury two or three at a time in shallow holes.

A squirrel cuts four large cones from a pine tree. When they have fallen to the ground, he scurries down the trunk and begins shelling the nuts. Hulls scatter around him. As he shells the kernels, he runs first one way, then another, to hide them. By an uncanny sense of smell, he can find his buried treasures. Even when their hiding places are covered with snow, the squirrel smells them out and digs down and under the drifts to get them.

A marmot emerges from her den under the rock pile and climbs to the top. She sits in the sun, looking in every direction for enemy signs.

No bobcat, mountain lion, or coyote is anywhere near. Down runs the marmot to eat the still-green grass at the edges of logs. She stays close to her burrow, running only to the edge of the burned place. The marmot eats and eats, as if she will never get enough, then, thoroughly stuffed, climbs slowly back to sun herself on the rocks.

Long before snowfall, this last marmot in the rock pile

will be layered with fat. She will be the first animal to crawl into her burrow to sleep until spring. The fat over her body will keep the marmot alive and healthy until green grass grows again.

From the forest near the mountain emerges the female bear, the same bear who came early in spring bringing her cubs. Wary, but sluggish, intent on finding more food, she stops beside some flat stones near the beaver dam. Her strong front claws turn the stones, then the bear licks up insects. Down the stream she waddles.

Beside a chokecherry thicket, the old bear stops. Grunting, she pulls the branches down and strips the crimson fruit—leaves, twigs, and cherries together—and stuffs them into her greedy mouth.

Two more bears shuffle into the meadow—the cubs. They are nearly grown, only slightly smaller than their mother. The young bears keep a respectful distance. Weaned and on their own, lessons learned, from this time forward the cubs must behave as adult bears.

Mother bear walks up the stream to the trout pool. The sun stands high in the sky. The air is still. The bear pants as she walks, mouth open, tongue hanging. A thick layer of fat and a heavy, dark fur coat blanket her body. She wades into the pool, rolling, grunting, splashing. The cold water relieves her itching hot skin. She climbs up the bank, shakes her dripping bulk, and ambles into the woods.

Bears, like other hibernating animals, store up great quantities of body fat. From this they live while they sleep. Thick fur coats protect them from winter's cold.

The insects prepare, too. In autumn some kinds of

A chokecherry branch with ripe fruit.

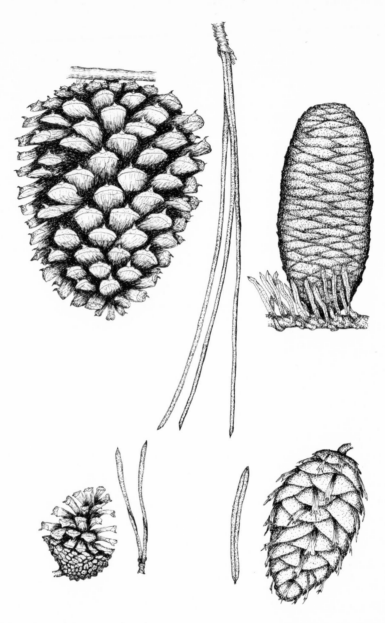

Various kinds of cones: At the upper left is a ripe cone of ponderosa pine, with its three-to-a-bundle long needles beside it. At upper right is a cone of white fir on its branch, with single short needles. At lower left is a lodgepole pine cone and a two-needle bundle. At the lower right is a Douglas fir cone and its single needles.

butterflies and moths lay eggs, which they hide under logs or on the protected sides of rocks. These eggs remain dormant, in an inactive state, until warm spring days cause them to hatch. Still other insects burrow into the ground and live in a sleeping condition until spring.

Crickets dig into the soil and lay their eggs, where they remain protected until spring hatching time. The parent insects die, but the species lives on.

Grasshoppers hide their eggs in gravel beds, leaving them to hatch new grasshoppers in the spring.

From the tallest tree at the edge of the meadow, to the tiniest flower beside the brook, plants prepare for winter.

Seeds fall to the earth, and lie covered with leaves and bits of soil; dormant, inactive, until spring awakens them to new growth.

Some plants not only produce seeds, but grow from the same roots year after year. These *perennial* plants have strong root systems that are not damaged by winter freezing. By autumn most of the green tops of these plants have dried, leaving the sturdy roots to start new growth next season. Even the fire could not kill all the roots of the perennials.

Frost touches the aspens below the beaver dam. Golden leaves shimmer in the sunlight, falling one by one, a gilt carpet over the meadow floor.

Red and brown chokecherry leaves drift to earth. Pale yellow willow leaves bob and float on the surface of the stream. The pines and firs at the edge of the meadow stand dark green, pale spring-growth tips hardened into stiff needles. Brown cones dot the dry grass beneath the trees.

In autumn the sap which runs under the bark of trees and shrubs, bringing water and nutrients up from the soil, slows its pace. Growth stops. Twigs harden as the trees make ready to withstand the cold winter.

Carpeting a quiet edge of the beaver pond, round water lily leaves, called pads, glisten in the sun. Something splashes among them at the edge of the water. There, sitting on a partly submerged log, a porcupine harvests lily pads and stuffs them into his mouth. Water lilies make a salad treat for this prickly barkeater. Soon the lilies will freeze, but now, while they still float on the pond, the porcupine feasts.

His appetite satisfied, the porcupine waddles toward the forest edge. His nest, under the roots of a half-dead pine, is only about fifty yards from the pond's edge. Prickly "Porky" doesn't like to travel. He moves only for food and then no farther than he must, for he is slow, lazy, and stupid.

A porcupine does not need to be swift or cunning. He needs no protective coloring, for he is armed with a coat that few predators of the woodland and meadow dare touch. Over the head, back, and sides of this giant rodent, a cousin of the mice, extends a layer of hollow, sharp, barbed spines, or quills. They stick into the noses of meddlesome foxes, bobcats, or coyotes, burying themselves cruelly into the flesh. Because of his prickly armor, a porcupine is afraid of no one.

A porcupine's best weapon of defense is his tail: wide,

The porcupine climbs into a pine tree.

flat, about half the length of his body, and covered with sharp quills. Whenever he is molested, he thrashes this cruel tail from side to side. Any animal who does not jump out of a porcupine's way will be sorry indeed.

Contrary to old superstition, a porcupine cannot throw his quills. They stick into the flesh of any creature who is foolish enough to touch them and are easily detached from the porcupine's body.

Chattering his bright orange teeth, the porcupine reaches the trees. He climbs slowly up the trunk of a pine. There he will sit, all day and night, maybe for three or four days, napping and eating bark. This tree and others nearby have been severely damaged by the hungry, gnawing porcupines. They chew off the outer protective bark layers and sometimes kill large trees.

Porcupines live almost entirely on bark. During summer, they eat some green plants. Along with their diet of bark and plants, they like salt. In search of salt, porcupines make themselves pests around camps. They gnaw anything that has salt on it. Campers who leave axes or other tools with wood handles in reach of the spiny nibblers have found them severely chewed. Salt from human hands is the lure that tempts the porcupines.

One summer, an ecologist and his wife lived at a meadow's edge in the Adirondack Mountains. One night they were awakened by sounds of gnawing, grunting, and sniffling. They bounded from bed, grabbed a flashlight, and opened the cabin door. There stood a huge porcupine. He wobbled down the porch steps out of the light. Around the doorknob, a great gnawed circle marked the place where he had chewed the salty wood.

Porcupines mate in autumn, then go their separate ways to find winter dens. They do not hibernate, but doze most of the winter. In early spring the young are born: one prickly baby, or sometimes two. Mother porcupine takes complete charge of her offspring. Father goes his solitary way, chewing, grunting, sleeping.

In the aspen grove below the beaver pond, a tree

crashes with the swish and crackle of breaking limbs. The beavers are busy, back in their pond working feverishly to repair the dam and lay in a great store of bark for winter food.

Swimming beaver heads arrow the smooth surface of the pond. With a resounding slap of his tail, one big beaver warns his tribe that danger is in the meadow. Down they dive, paddling rapidly with webbed hind feet. Then, one by one, they raise their heads to look. The men who caused the alarm are leaving in their noisy truck. The beavers waddle up the slippery bank toward the aspen grove.

A big beaver selects a tree with a six-inch trunk. Using his broad flat tail for a prop, he sits upright, balanced against the tree with his short front feet. He gnaws at the white aspen trunk, woodchips flying from his sharp teeth. When the big beaver has cut a deep notch, he moves to the other side. Crunching echoes over the meadow. The careful logger chews around the whole tree trunk, gauging his cut like a skillful lumberjack, so that the tree will fall toward the pond.

The aspen topples with a crush of branches. The beaver begins to cut it into short sections. Two other beavers come to chew off limbs. Then, piece by piece, they drag the fallen tree down a muddy slide and out into the water.

The beavers sink the tree pieces to the bottom of the pond where they store them for winter food. They use part of the limbs and sticks to repair holes in the beaver dam.

If the dam is sound, the water level is always high. Deep water keeps the beavers safe from predators. Under

The beavers work feverishly to repair their dam.

the pond water, they store tree pieces from which they eat the bark. Deep water protects the submerged door to the beaver lodge.

Some of the beavers work on the mound-shaped lodge. It rises above the surface of the pond like a giant mud-and-stick bubble. Some beavers bring small branches to add to its surface, while others dive to the bottom and come up with front paws full of mud. This is the plaster, which holds the sticks together. One beaver places his mud on the wood frame, then turns around, and with a resounding whack of his broad flat tail, flattens it and smooths it into place.

The floor of the beaver house is on a raised platform of sticks above the water level. A slanting entry from underneath secures this home from invaders. A beaver lodge is both dry and safe.

The beaver's hairless tail is a marvelous tool. He uses it for a plasterer's trowel, a lumberman's prop, a boatman's rudder, and as a noisemaker to warn of danger.

All day long the beavers work, cutting, dragging, sinking pieces of the aspen trees. They dive, plaster, waddle up the banks. They work into the night, for they must hurry. Winter will soon be upon them, when the frozen surface of the pond will become a prison, as well as a safeguard from danger.

Beavers, with their amazing engineering works, change the meadow. They cut the aspens and make more open space. They dam the creek to provide a watery home for fish, frogs, water plants, and insects. Often, when a large beaver colony lives for many years in one meadow, they exhaust the supply of aspens and alders and move to an-other meadow to find fresh supplies. When that happens, the carefully-kept dam gradually falls apart. The stream rushes through, draining the pond. The water table in the meadow falls so that different plants come to live there. Perhaps forest trees move into the open space to turn the meadow to woodland.

At the west side of the meadow, the deer browse, searching for leaves that are not yet autumn-dry. Five of them cluster around a clump of deer brush: two does, a half-grown fawn, a small buck, and, off to one side by him-self, the old wide-antlered male.

Silently, from the shelter of the trees on the upwind side of the deer, creep two men. They carry rifles. Hunters have come to the meadow.

The deer eat steadily, for they cannot smell the men, nor have they seen them. One hunter aims. A shot cracks, echoing against the trees and mountains. His neck spurting crimson blood, the young buck falls. He struggles—lies still.

The hunters rush to the fallen deer, talking, excited. One man hurries downstream and out of the meadow.

Soon he returns, driving a pickup truck. Together the two men load the dead deer and bounce down the meadow toward the valley.

The remaining deer snort their alarm and bound into the woods.

Suddenly, the meadow is quiet. Even the noisy jay sits like a stone on his branch. Every creature fears, above all others, that intruder called man.

But the hunter, like the carnivores, helps to maintain the balance between deer and their food supply. If there were no hunters to kill the deer, some would starve because there would be too few browse plants for all of them. Cruel as he may seem, the hunter plays a useful part in keeping plants and animals in balance.

A dark cloud covers the mountain top. Slowly it spreads over the whole sky, gray, menacing. A fresh breeze whispers down the mountain. Huge snowflakes float to earth. Slowly at first, then faster and faster, the wet snow falls on trees, grass, and rocks. The meadow turns from brown and green to white.

Night falls on a snow-covered world.

A black, white, and gray chickadee sings his defiance to winter.

8

The Meadow Sleeps Again

Morning sun lights a sparkling mountain world. Grass blades lie flattened under the wet snow. The cold whiteness clings to the willows, bends the pine and fir branches downward, covers the black burn scar. Winter softens the meadow's outlines and quiets its sounds.

Where the creek leaves the forest, the female bear appears. She walks straight across and into the trees, hurrying to her den to sleep away the cold months.

A huge male bear crosses in the opposite direction. He is the female's mate, seeking his winter cave at the foot of the mountain. Bear tracks dent the snow.

Each bear hibernates separately. The autumn mating season has passed. Sometime, during the long dark hours of hibernation, the female bear will give birth to one or two tiny blind cubs. She will nurse them in her den, then, when their eyes have opened, will bring them out to the meadow with the first warm spring days.

Four deer enter the meadow; two does, the big buck, and a nearly-grown fawn. They crop twigs and a few clinging leaves from the deer brush at the edge of the forest, then wander down the stream. They nibble around the willow thicket, move slowly past the beaver dam, and down toward the valley.

The deer will spend the cold months in the lower country where there is little snow. There they will live until spring returns.

As the deer leave the meadow, two gray figures emerge from the woods. The coyotes follow the deer. Stealthily they wind in and out between trees and bushes, careful not to show themselves to the deer. Hunting will be easier in the lower valley. Perhaps one of those deer will weaken. Then the coyotes can catch him. Silently, they follow.

Slowly, over the past week, the flycatchers flew away from the meadow, closely followed by peewees.

The nuthatches move down the mountain, for seeds and insects will be easier to find in warmer valleys. The bird caroling of spring is silenced.

The sledgehammer drilling of the giant pileated woodpecker breaks the snowy silence.

Jays squawk and scold, for these noisemakers stay in the winter meadow.

A thin ice glaze extends out nearly to the center of the beaver pond. One mallard drake swims in a circle, the last of his clan to stay in the cold water. He stretches his iridescent green and purple neck. A sound of excited quacking echoes from the sky. The lone mallard flaps his wings and rises from the water to join his fellows in their southward migration.

The beavers work on, even though snow mantles the aspen grove. They swim in the narrowing pond water, diving, bringing up mud, and plastering their lodge. Each layer of mud added during the day freezes at night. When ice covers all the pond, the beavers will have a warm, safe, thick-walled home for the winter.

Beavers and many other animals grow heavy fur coats to protect them from the cold. The bear goes to his den wearing a thick warm fur. The fox's fur grows dense to insulate him from winter chills. The coyote's fur grows long. The black and white skunk waddles like a rolling ball in his bulky winter garments. So it is with all the animals. Each has his own special protection against freezing weather.

Even with extra fur in winter, many animals suffer from cold. But worse than cold is starvation. With most plants covered, and animals either hibernated or gone from the meadow, there is little to eat for those who remain. Hunting for food becomes a full-time job for many of the snow-dwellers.

Snow protects the meadow mice. They build tunnels through the white silences. Down next to the soil, where dead meadow grasses cover the earth, the mice make little grass huts, or nests, where they sleep.

Out from the security of his grass house, a tiny white-footed mouse scampers down his snow tunnel. He remembers something. His nose twitches, smelling the faint odor of grass seeds. He runs on. There they are. He stops at a widened place in his tunnel to nose tiny seeds from the wet tangle of dead grass stems. There are only six seeds, but

Mice build tunnels and grass nests under the snow. This diagram shows a cross-section through the snow with a white-footed mouse, its tunnel and round grass nest.

six will keep him alive until he can find more. He crops a few brown grass stems, then scurries back to his nest to rest. When there is so little to eat, he must rest often. If he rests, he needs less food for energy.

As the tiny mouse nears the door of his grass nest, he hesitates a moment. His whiskers twitch. Danger? He sits very still, listening. Not a sound ripples his snowy world. The mouse darts into his hut.

A sudden terrified squeak, a hiss, then silence returns to the mouse tunnel. A short-tailed weasel waited to ambush the homecoming mouse.

Wearing their snow-colored white winter fur, short-tailed weasels live almost entirely upon mice. Zoologists studying the habits of these weasels sometimes find them in grass mouse nests completely lined with the fur of their victims.

Animals such as mice often reproduce rapidly. When this happens, the numbers of mice increase to the point where there are too many for them all to survive. They may die in great numbers because there is not enough food. Or disease may infest the closely-packed colonies and kill many of them. When this happens, the animal populations drop sharply, almost mysteriously, leaving only the strongest to begin to build the race again.

This cyclic buildup and disappearance of populations may happen with grasshoppers, pocket gophers, deer— any insect or animal that increases to great numbers.

Pocket gophers continue to work during cold winter months. They make burrows as in summer, but closer to the soil surface. The gophers push earth out of their tunnels to make cores, long cylinders of soil which appear like wandering snakes on the surface of the meadow when snow melts in the spring.

Out from the treetops flies a gray bird. He sails over the meadow, light barred wings outspread, then drops bulletlike to the snowy earth. A screech, a struggle, and the goshawk stands on the limp body of a snowshoe hare. Rumpling the blood-spattered snow, the hawk tears his victim apart. He eats, discarding fur and bones. Then, stomach heavy, this fiercest of birds sails slowly into the sky crying a contented "Kak, kak, kak."

On a fir tree at the west side of the meadow, two cheerful little birds chirp and chatter. The gay black, white, and gray chickadees sing their defiance of winter and snow. They hop through the trees hunting tiny hidden insects or insect eggs. Gay birds, the short-tailed, fat-bodied chickadees add a joyous note to the solemn whiteness of winter.

"Chick-a-dee-dee-deeee," they call to each other as they hop and flutter through the snow-draped trees.

Along the creek, dried brown yarrow heads stand stiff above the snow, reminders that summer flowers bloomed here not long ago.

The high meadow as it is today, is an ever-changing community of plants, animals, and man, influenced by weather and fire. The surrounding forest is constantly crowding in, turning meadowland to woodland. If the beaver should leave the meadow and the pond should drain, then the water level in the meadow soil would drop, making a more favorable habitat for forest trees.

Deer crop the brush at the meadow edges and keep it from crowding over all the grassland.

Small rodents—mice, gophers, ground squirrels—cultivate the meadow soil, making it more suitable for grass than for trees. They help keep the meadow as it is.

An occasional fire also helps to keep the meadow open. It burns the brush and small tree seedlings around the edges. Burning releases the minerals stored in live plants and plant debris on the meadow floor. These minerals provide extra fertilizer to boost plant growth.

Spring, summer, autumn, winter, the mountain meadow is a special place, exactly the right habitat for the

The goshawk stands on the dead body of the snowshoe hare.

animals which live there and the plants which grow in its sunny open space. People delight in the meadow, a place to camp, picnic, fish, hunt and relax, a place to enjoy the forest.

Now it is winter, snow-locked and silent. But spring will come again to the meadow. The frozen creek will awake to ripple in the sunshine. Birds will return, migrating up the mountain to build their nests and rear their young. Deer will browse, trout will leap again. Then, man, too, will return to the meadow to camp beside the stone fireplace above the beaver pond.

Another cloud darkens the mountain top. Slowly the

whole sky grays. The sun dims, disappears. Snow falls, covering the bloody traces of the goshawk's kill, silencing the jay's raucous cry. For three hours and more, white flakes drift to earth, then slowly, as day darkens into night, the snowfall stops.

As darkness claims the meadow, from his perch on the half-dead pine, the great horned owl calls, "Whoo-whoo-whooo."

Soft snow muffles the sound of weighted branches as they snap and fall to earth. The brook flows silently, its tongue frozen, while overhead, the last wedge of geese cries its way southward.

Bibliography

Bonner, J., and Galston, A. W., *Principles of Plant Physiology*. San Francisco, W. H. Freeman Co., 1952.

Chapman, R. N., *Animal Ecology*. New York, McGraw-Hill, Inc., 1931.

Clarke, F. E., *Wild Animals*. New York, The Macmillan Company, 1939.

Daubenmire, R., *Plant Communities*. New York, Harper and Row, Publishers, 1968.

Emmons, W. H., Thiel, G. A., Stauffer, C. R., and Allison, I. S., *Geology*. New York, McGraw-Hill, Inc., 1939.

Grosvenor, G., and Wetmore, W., *The Book of Birds, Vols. I and II*, Washington, D. C., National Geographic Society, 1932.

Irving, L., "Adaptation to Cold." *Scientific American*, Vol. 214, No. 1 (January, 1966), pp. 94–101.

Kelly, G. D., and Middlekauff, W. W., "Biological Studies of Dissostura Spurcata Saccssure." *Hilgardia, Journal of Agricultural Science*, Vol. 30, No. 14, Berkeley, U. of Calif. Exp. Sta., 1961.

Meyer, B. S., and Anderson, D. B., *Plant Physiology*. Princeton, N.J., D. Van Nostrand Co., Inc., 1939.

Mills, E. A., *In Beaver World*. New York, Houghton Mifflin Company, 1913.

Murie, A., "Ecology of the Coyote in the Yellowstone." Nat'l Park Svc., Fauna Series #4, Washington, D.C., U. S. Govt. Printing Office, 1940.

Odum, E. P., and Odum, H. T., *Fundamentals of Ecology*. Philadelphia, W. B. Saunders Company, 1953.

Pruitt, W. O., Jr., "Animals in the Snow." *Scientific American*, Vol. 202, No. 1 (January, 1966) pp. 60–68.

Seton, E. T., *Life Histories of Northern Animals*. Vols. I–IV, New York, Charles Scribner's Sons, 1909.

Skinner, M. P., *Bears in the Yellowstone*. Chicago, A. C. McClurg, 1925.

Storer, T. I., and Usinger, R. L., *Sierra Nevada Natural History*. Berkeley, University of California Press, 1963.

Weaver, J. E., and Clements, F. E., *Plant Ecology*. New York, McGraw Hill, Inc., 1935.

Index

The Authors

ELEANOR B. HEADY was born in Bliss, Idaho, and attended the University of Idaho where she received a B.A. in English. She taught English and drama for a year before her marriage, and since then she has worked for several radio stations doing announcing and storytelling for children's programs.

HAROLD F. HEADY was born and grew up on a farm in Buhl, Idaho, and he received a B.S. in Forestry from the University of Idaho, an M.S. in Botany from the New York State College of Forestry, and a PhD. in Plant Ecology from the University of Nebraska.

Mr. Heady is a professor of Range Management and Plant Ecology at the University of California at Berkeley, and his own research in this field has carried him to East Africa, Australia, New Zealand, and Saudi Arabia.

Both of the Headys belong to the California Writer's Club. Mr. Heady has written numerous books and articles on range management, and Mrs. Heady has written several other books for young people. While traveling with her husband in Kenya, East Africa, she gathered material for her collection of African folk tales, *Jambo, Sungura,* and while in Africa and Australia she gathered information for *Coat of the Earth: The Story of Grass,* for which Mr. Heady provided outstanding botanical illustrations of grasses.

The Headys have a son and a daughter, and they now make their home in Berkeley, California.

Cover design by Antoinette Nici